# My Life With The Stars

## Best, Ali and the Panties!

Tony Flood

First published in the UK in April 2012 by MyVoice Publishing

Copyright: © Tony Flood
Tony Flood asserts the moral right to be identified as the author of this work

Published by: MyVoice Publishing,
Unit 1,
16 Maple Road,
Eastbourne,
BN23 6NY

ISBN: 978-0-9569682-5-8

All rights reserved. No part of this publication may be reproduced without the permission of the author, stored in a retrieval system, or transmitted, in any form or by any means, electronic, mechanical, photocopying, recording or otherwise, without the permission of the publisher.

This book is sold subject to the condition that it shall not, by way of trade or otherwise, be lent, re-sold, hired out or otherwise circulated without the publisher's prior consent in any form of binding or cover other than that in which it is published and without a similar condition including this condition being imposed on the subsequent purchaser.

# DEDICATIONS

This book is dedicated to the memory of my parents Mabel and Dennis Flood and my wonderful grandparents Winnie and Reggie Burwash, who brought me up with love and kindness.

They, together with my lovely wife Heather and son James, have been an inspiration to me as a writer.

I would like to thank Dec Cluskey of The Bachelors, actresses Susie Amy, June Whitfield and Shirley Anne Field, actors Daniel Hill and Denis Lill, former Manchester United manager Tommy Docherty and journalists Sami Mokbel, Dale Harry and John Payne for their supportive reviews.

Thanks also to Barry King, Ted Cassell, Jeff Klepper, Graham Dunn, Jeff Morton, Brian Francis, Tricia Sneath and others for providing pictures, some of which are used in this book.

Special thanks go to publisher Rex Sumner for his considerable efforts in steering the book through the choppy seas of production, printing and distribution.

# REVIEWS

*If you want to know the ins and outs of showbiz, sport, films and politics this is the one! Tony Flood takes us on a riotous trip through the years of chatting with so many of the great names...George Best, Muhammad Ali, Frankie Howerd etc. Check out the Sir John Gielgud story - my personal favourite. There is something magical in hearing the frailties of the huge names... Sir Ralph Richardson forgetting his lines! The present day guys? How Tony will be sued for his Redknapp stories? I jest... he has all the latest shenanigans and the ancient stuff... the kids will love it and so will the old timers. I just love a good yarn and Tony's book is full of them, including my Beatles story.* **- DEC CLUSKEY, THE BACHELORS.**

*As a former Fleet Street journalist and Sky Television executive, Tony Flood has been able to put together a host of revealing anecdotes and interviews involving big name celebrities in My Life With The Stars. Sports fans and show business followers will enjoy reading about star names ranging from Muhammad Ali, Bobby Moore and George Best to Frank Sinatra, The Beatles and Bruce Forsyth. So happy page turning!* **- JUNE WHITFIELD, actress.**

*My Life With The Stars is full of cheeky anecdotes, and is perfect for fans of entertainment and sport. It's packed with stories and tales from Tony's life, and the diverse and fascinating people who he has met along the way. I love reading about George Best, a man that I, too, was lucky enough to meet.* **- SUSIE AMY, actress.**

*Tony Flood reveals some fascinating secrets about top sports stars in his excellent new book. It contains great stories about Liverpool manager Kenny Dalglish, George Best and Muhammad Ali that make riveting - and very amusing - reading. My Life With The Stars is a well written and comprehensively researched book, which also gives a new insight into many of the scandals that have gone on in the world of sport, show business and newspapers, including those happening this year. And there are some knock-out quotes from Harry Redknapp and yours truly. This book should appeal to everyone, men and women, young and old. Once you start reading it you can't put it down.* **- TOMMY DOCHERTY, *former Manchester United manager.***

*I much enjoyed reading the many anecdotes in Tony Flood's book, and those people with a love of show business or sport should find this a great read. I am very happy to endorse My Life With the Stars.* **- SHIRLEY ANNE FIELD, actress.**

*Tony Flood's dealings with Muhammad Ali, George Best, Bobby Moore and Kenny Dalglish, plus a host of showbiz celebrities, make fascinating reading. WOW! So many of their secrets now come out! The most gripping interview was Tony's exclusive with former Liverpool goalkeeper Bruce Grobbelaar the day after the Hillsborough disaster, the deadliest stadium-related tragedy in British history. Revealing how Grobbelaar tried to help dying fans while the match was still being played was a remarkable story. -* **SAMI MOKBEL, *Daily Mail sports writer.***

*Retired tabloid journalist Tony Flood has compiled a wonderful list of anecdotes, featuring a galaxy of stars from the worlds of sport, entertainment and politics. There's Bill Clinton's none-too-subtle chat-up lines, Carly Simon's inadvertent public spanking and George Best's horde of female followers. Tales, too, of theatrical Knights Richardson, Geilgud and my own hero, Olivier. My 'Murder on the Nile' co-star Kate O'Mara also makes a revealing appearance! Quite a read! -* **DENIS LILL, *actor.***

*Tony Flood has the knack of instantly finding a connection with people he meets and telling a great story. He's also a very, very funny guy - and all these qualities are the ingredients that make My Life With The Stars a real page-turner. I had looked forward to reading revelations about sport legends such as Muhammad Ali, George Best, Freddie Flintoff and Bobby Charlton - and I wasn't disappointed. Tony has scooped the whole of Fleet Street and his great stories revealing secrets about showbiz stars Elvis Presley, Frank Sinatra, Peter Sellers, The Beatles and Tom Jones are equally startling. My Life With The Stars is a superbly entertaining read and I strongly recommend it.* **- DALE HARRY, *Sport Publications Project Manager, Inside the Games.***

*As a sports journalist, I have met many larger-than-life characters and it is fair to say that Tony was the largest. Some journalists (myself included) tend to be a little bit awe-struck when they talk to the rich and famous - but often these big names would be awe-struck when they spoke to Tony! He was totally fearless. I'm not sure any other journalist on this planet would have been brave enough to tell Martin Allen, the former Brentford manager whose nickname 'Mad Dog' was surely more reality than affection, that he had got his tactics wrong. I always felt Tony had a great book in him.* **- JOHN PAYNE, *sports editor and writer.***

# CONTENTS

# PREFACE

I've interviewed or chatted to a galaxy of stars during my long career as a journalist, television executive, author and theatre critic.

They have come from most areas of the entertainment business, but the biggest names and most charismatic characters have been George Best and Muhammad Ali.

Meeting my two super heroes was a great privilege and also brought me into contact with two glamorous ladies who were offering to have sex with them!

One was so desperate that she gave me an item of her underwear to pass on to Bestie.

This curvy blonde pushed into my hand her pink G-string, with the waistband tied to a room key, and asked me to give it to George, who was tantalisingly out of her reach in a VIP area where I had been talking to him before paying a brief visit to the loo.

The other lady, a frustrated brunette, prevented from getting near to Ali because of his large entourage around him, was a little more refined. She gave a security guard an envelope to pass to Ali, and when the guard opened it in front of me it contained a nude photo of her dangling her panties on her forefinger, with a phone number written on the back.

But more about that later!

Other sports stars did not seem to have the same effect on the ladies, but I had some fascinating interviews with footballers Sir Stanley Matthews, Sir Tom Finney and Sir Bobby Charlton, boxers Frank Bruno, Henry Cooper and Nigel Benn, golfers Sandy Lyle and Tony Jacklin and tennis player Monica Seles. And there have been differences of opinion with Kenny Dalglish and Alan Curbishley which I will also tell you about later.

I've come across many comedians in my time, among them men who actually intend to be funny such as Jimmy Carr, Joe Pasquale, Harry Hill, Al Murray, Mike Reid, Frank Skinner, Frankie Howerd and the legendary Max Miller.

The most delightful actresses I've met have been June Whitfield, Shirley Anne Field, Susan Penhaligon, Linda Gray from 'Dallas', Patsy Kensit, Kate O'Mara, and the lovely Joanne Heywood and Susie Amy.

June is a real sweetie, who rarely has a bad word to say about anyone, but she does explain in this book why her demanding television partner Terry Scott could give some actors a difficult time.

Britt Ekland was polite when I interviewed her, but not very forthcoming, so I felt less

Tony gets a helping hand from Patsy Kensit

comfortable talking to her than I was the other actresses I've mentioned, particularly the charming Susie Amy, who forgave me for unintentionally calling her by her surname.

"So many people make the mistake of thinking my first name is Amy," said the 'Footballers

Wives' star.

A sex symbol who did not send my pulse racing was Abi Titmuss (as bright as a button, pleasant and admittedly attractive, but not the glamour girl I had expected).

Singers I have most enjoyed chatting to are Dec Cluskey of the Bachelors, Petula Clark, Clare Sweeney, Cher, Mark Wynter (now an actor), Max Bygraves and Anita Harris...the list goes on! But, sadly, old age has caught up with Petula, at 79, and Bygraves, who is 10 years her senior!

Funnily enough, a young Max Bygraves used to sing in the public house run by my grandparents in Woolwich, South East London, long before he was famous. I met him years later in Yarmouth and reminded him about it, but I omitted to tell him that, after hearing him perform in their pub, my grandparents didn't think he would ever become a star!

I actually turned down the chance to meet Cheryl Cole and her then husband Ashley because I simply do not like the way they have sometimes acted and spoken in public.

I have not met Frank Sinatra, The Beatles, Joan Collins or Peter Sellers, either, but I have some great stories to tell about them in this book thanks to my other contacts in the world of show business. I will be revealing Sinatra's darker side, why Paul McCartney peed on his rival's shoes, how Joan Collins' words led to co-star Kate O'Mara being axed from 'Dynasty' and why Sellers made his wife Britt Ekland squirm with embarrassment.

During my time as Controller of Information at Sky Television, I had to sort out various problems, two of which concerned snooker star Jimmy White and football manager Ron Atkinson (more details later!).

Most days at Sky I was rubbing shoulders with the likes of Lennox Lewis, Ryder Cup golfer Brian Barnes, Roger Black, who won 4x400metre relay gold medals at both the World and European Championships, World snooker champion Dennis Taylor and Eurosport's head of programmes Adrian Metcalfe, a former Olympic Games athlete.

I also interviewed on camera Jimmy White, Stephen Hendry and Barry Hearn while helping to organise one of Sky and Eurosport's biggest sports events, the first World Snooker Masters.

I cannot claim that these stars became big buddies of mine, because they didn't, although I frequently mixed with Bobby Moore when I was his boss at the notorious down-market tabloid Sunday Sport.

Indeed, a few of the celebrities I met might not even remember my name because I interviewed some of them only once and I was not a famous columnist, although I wrote by-lined double-page spreads for the Daily Mirror, Sunday Mirror and Daily Star as a freelance.

I spent several years of my career in executive roles as Editor of Football Monthly magazine, Controller of Information at Sky Television, Sports Editor of the Lancashire Evening Telegraph Series and, of course, Head of Sport at Sunday Sport and later Fleet Street News Agency.

But at the news agency I was in effect a freelance writer who earned by-lines with various national, regional and weekly newspapers, I obtained interviews with many big name stars and snatched quotes from others, usually either before or after top sports events, and there are some great anecdotes to recall!

I even got invited to put my hand on the bare thigh of 'Strictly Come Dancing's Miss Whiplash, Erin Boag!

Oh, and I've not even mentioned my recent brush with royalty, have I?

They don't come much more famous than the lady with the corgis, do they?

I actually met her in 2011, and I'm the only one to have been cheeky enough to say to her: "Your majesty, how long have you been impersonating Jeannette Charles?"

But it was look-alike Jeannette Charles, dressed as the Queen, to whom I was speaking - NOT The Queen herself!

Jeannette has a great sense of humour and gave me a ticking off, telling me: "You are a most disrespectful subject."

In addition to working as a television public relations executive at Sky, my career as a journalist over more than 45 years included an enjoyable spell as editor of Football Monthly, Britain's oldest football magazine. I later worked on the staff of national Sunday tabloid paper The People part-time until September, 2010 when I finally retired.

There have also been appearances on radio and television, including featuring regularly on BBC News 24 as a sports pundit - if you missed me that was because they stuck me on at 6.30 in the morning!

I have been given some interesting missions as a writer, including acting as a stand-up comedian! I was able to tell my audience that I was the first journalist in the family, in stark contrast to my great grandfather, who was a floor stainer - he didn't mean to be, but as he got older he couldn't help himself! Boom, boom!

Other journalistic tasks saw me take dancing lessons from the delightful Erin Boag, climb the Great Wall of China, organise and judge a beauty competition and play football with George Best and Bobby Moore.

Scoring a goal against a star-studded team which included Ossie Ardiles and Steve Coppell has got to be a highlight.

Ironically, since retiring to Eastbourne I have got

to know two of Britain's most iconic stars Dec Cluskey of The Bachelors and actress Shirley Anne Field.

Both are lovely people, as is Dec's wife Sandy, a former dancer on many television shows.

Dec kindly introduced the film premiere of the comedy play I wrote called 'Hacking It' when it was shown for the first time at the Winter Garden Theatre, Eastbourne in January this year, and Shirley Anne sent a wonderful 'good luck' message to be read out to the audience.

Apart from Muhammad Ali, I have not come across anyone who lights up a room more quickly than the charismatic Mr. Cluskey.

But let me start by telling you about the man, who for me, was the greatest player and playboy in the world!

CHAPTER ONE

# GEORGE BEST AND THE G-STRING

I met George Best a couple of times socially and on the second occasion I was given the task by one of his sexy female admirers of handing to him her G-string, wrapped around a key, so that she could lure him into her bedroom.

But my biggest memory of Best was playing with him in a benefit match for former Charlton Athletic goal-scoring hero Derek Hales. I will relate this amusing story first and come to the foxy lady shortly!

My appearance with the Irish genius was also memorable for another Charlton player, Steve Gritt, who later became the club's joint manager. Gritt wrote in the club programme: "It was a massive coup to get George along. The one thing I remember about the game was that a local reporter called Tony Flood came on at half-time and followed George around for 45 minutes. It was like he was shadow-marking him - but they were on the same team!"

That's how much in awe of Best I was at the time!

He had lost his acceleration, but I was able to see his magic footwork at close hand as he glided past opponents as if they weren't there. It was a master class in ball control and, needless to say, there were several goals created or scored that day by the former Manchester United legend, arguably the greatest player of his era.

I don't think I contributed much, apart from one 'golden' moment. I actually played a return pass to Best to help set up one of the goals, which left me well chuffed! I was so grateful to the organiser Michael La Roche for inviting me to play in this star-studded match at Welling United's ground on May 5, 1985, simply on the basis that I was reasonably well known locally as a journalist who covered Charlton's matches.

My other team-mates and I saw Best naked in the dressing room and showers afterwards - and he still looked in pretty good shape to us, even though he was well past his prime.

But my admiration for George was nothing compared to what the ladies felt for him. I was present on another occasion when a leggy lady went to great lengths to try to get him into her bed.

We were at a plush hotel where I chatted to George in a 'VIP area' which was out of bounds to this very attractive, elegantly dressed woman who called "Hello, George" in a deliciously soft voice. All she got from Bestie was a smile, but that did not deter her.

This gorgeous blonde, in her thirties, watched me go to the loo and presumably she quickly visited the 'ladies' at the same time. When I

George Best with team-mate Tony and his son James

came out of the 'gents' she was waiting for me. She pressed herself against me, pushed something into my hand and purred seductively with that wonderful voice: "Give this to George - tell him it's from the blonde he smiled at." When I looked I found she had given me her bright pink G-string, with the waistband tied around a room key.

Without a trace of embarrassment she smiled at me mischievously, and then added: "Tell him I've just taken it off."

George just laughed about such incidents and revealed that so many women propositioned him each week that he lost count. But later that night I spotted him walking purposefully towards the hotel lifts with what looked like the pink G-string in his hand.

This illustrates just how much of a magnet Best was to the women - even when he was no longer playing. At least he then had no obligations to any club and was free to do what he liked. Unfortunately, his sex romps were probably even more frequent during the time he was supposed to be at peak fitness at Manchester United.

The worst example of his sexual exploits came when he was caught in the act by his manager Wilf McGuinness at the team's hotel on the afternoon of Manchester United's FA Cup semi-final against Leeds in 1970.

An attractive woman had caught Best's eye on the hotel's stairs and he wasted no time in persuading her to go to his room.

McGuinness wanted to send him home, but Sir Matt Busy persuaded his young successor to let Best play - against Wilf's better judgement.

"George had an absolute nightmare of a game," McGuinness recalled. "We drew 0-0 and George missed the chance to win it for us by falling over the ball in front of goal."

Four years later Best's womanising led to him being charged with theft.

George was photographed leaving London society club Tramp with reigning Miss World Marjorie Wallace, then engaged to Formula One racing driver Peter Revson.

Apparently Best and Miss Wallace had a row and he returned to Manchester without her. At 3 am he was arrested and brought back to London's Wood Lane police station, where he was charged with burglary of her flat and the theft of a £2,000 mink coat, jewellery and spirits. Wallace was stripped of her title and Best advised that he could go to jail if he was found guilty.

But five days before Best was due in court, Revson was killed in practice for the South African Grand Prix on March 22. Wallace flew back to the States and the case was dropped.

I felt sorry for George because, as he confided, temptation was constantly put in front of him everywhere he went - something which his Manchester United team-mates Bobby Charlton, Denis Law & Co. were not exposed to in the same way.

Girls screamed whenever George made a personal appearance, and we had to stop them from molesting him at the testimonial football match!

Older women were also smitten by him. Actress Barbara Windsor, famous for her big boobs and saucy roles in the 'Carry On' films, was one of them.

She explained how females of all ages were captivated by his amazing sex appeal, which was nothing short of animal magnetism.

Barbara, who freely admitted having 'a magic moment' with Best, asked challengingly when interviewed by Piers Morgan: "How many women would have said 'no' to him? He was so beautiful.

"I met him at the premiere of a 'Carry On' in Manchester. In the bar afterwards he came over to me and I told him: 'Don't waste your time with me, darling, when all those lovely ladies are after you'.

"He said: 'When do I ever get to talk to someone like you?' Well, that did it. So that was it, a 'magic moment' again."

Barbara, who also had flings with Maurice Gibb from the Bee Gees, co-star Sid James and notorious gangsters Reggie and Charlie Kray, did not go into detail about her experience with Bestie. But she added: "He was fabulous!"

Best liked women of all shapes and sizes and Barbara was certainly all shapes and sizes! The actress was only 4ft 11in tall, but had a 38 inch bust, of which she says: "I wasn't always the confident, feisty blonde that I am today - two of my greatest assets were the bane of my life.

George, who started out as a tongue-tied shy lad from Belfast but rapidly grew in confidence, liked to share some great anecdotes. My favourite was when he was staying in a hotel and a bellboy delivered some champagne to his room where George was entertaining a scantily-

clad Miss World on a bed covered with his winnings from a casino.
The bellboy asked him: "Mr. Best, where did it all go wrong?"
George had such an impish sense of humour. The Manchester United idol, who drove his managers mad with his disappearing acts, admitted: "I used to go missing a lot - Miss Canada, Miss United Kingdom, Miss World..."
There was usually a touch of truth about his jokes. This was certainly the case when he confessed: "I spent 90 per cent of my money on women and drink - the rest I wasted!"

George Best and Tony

CHAPTER TWO

# FAN TOLD GROBBELAAR: 'THEY'RE KILLING US'

The most emotional story I ever wrote was when I obtained an exclusive interview with Liverpool goalkeeper Bruce Grobbelaar the day after the Hillsborough disaster which was the deadliest stadium-related tragedy in British history.

It resulted in the deaths of 96 people on April 15th, 1989 at the FA Cup semi-final between Liverpool and Nottingham Forest which was abandoned after six minutes.

Grobbelaar was choking back the tears as he told me how he was trying to take a goal kick when a fan yelled at him: "Bruce, help us. They're killing us."

Tony stands between two sporting icons, Seb Coe and Sir Bobby Charlton

The goalkeeper asked who was killing them and the man replied: "Our own fans - they are crushing us against the fences."

Grobbelaar had to ask the police to let supporters climb over the fences on to the areas surrounding the pitch while the game was still going on.

It was the most dramatic incident ever to happen during a major match.

The crush resulted from late-arriving Liverpool fans being allowed into the back of an already full stand at the Leppings Lane end of the ground.

Although the game was abandoned after six minutes, it was too late to save those who had been so severely crushed.

My exclusive interview with Grobbelaar made a double page spread in the Sunday Mirror.

Journalists need to be persistent without being too intrusive. An example of this was when I agreed to do an interview with Sir Bobby Charlton for the Daily Express on the 40th anniversary of the Munich Air Disaster.

Charlton was one of the survivors of the air crash which killed 23 people when the Manchester United team was travelling back from a European Cup match in Belgrade, Yugoslavia against Red Star on February 6th, 1958.

Bobby had given me his telephone number, but when I phoned him he said: "I'm sorry, Tony, but every year I get asked by journalists about this, and I'd rather not do an interview this time."

I was in a fix because the Daily Express was expecting 500 words from me. So I asked my wife Heather, who had no journalistic experience, to ring Bobby Charlton an hour later, saying she wanted to ask him some questions for a tribute article in memory of Jimmy Murphy, who had temporarily taken over the Manchester United team while manager Matt Busby was in hospital recovering from the plane crash.

I had written down six questions for Heather to put to him in the hope he would answer one or two of them. To my surprise Bobby gave full answers to all the questions, so I was able to write the article as a tribute to Murphy, which also, of course, reflected on the air crash.

Bobby was happy to pay tribute to Murphy - my only mistake was not giving Heather enough questions to ask him! He was warming to his theme when she had to cut the conversation short because she had run out of things to say!

Charlton recalled: "Jimmy Murphy kept the club afloat by cobbling together a team made up of reserves and loan players to help us complete our fixtures. Amazingly, against all odds, he got us to the FA Cup final.

"Jimmy was a big influence on me. He told me that if there was space ahead of me to take it by running with the ball, and that helped me to

score some of my most memorable goals."
This is typical of Bobby - always quick to thank those who had played a part in his huge success story!

CHAPTER THREE

# ALI AND THE NUDE PHOTO

Meeting Frank Bruno and Muhammad Ali were marvellous experiences and lots of fun!

I got to know Bruno, Britain's former heavyweight boxing champion, pretty well when I was Head of Sport at Sunday Sport in the late 1980's.

We were both going to the Sports Personality of the Year dinner where I was helping to entertain sports stars such as Nick Faldo and Frank himself because I was a member of the committee of the Sports Writers Association who were making the awards.

The amiable Bruno and I bumped into each other as we approached the Wembley venue.

Frank said to me: "Hello, Mr. Sunday Sport." Then he told me he was worried as he'd forgotten to bring his ticket. I assured Frank that it should not be a problem because the officials would let him in, especially as everyone would recognise him.

I was right on the first count but wrong on the second.

When we got to the reception area there was my date, a charming but perhaps on occasions a slightly 'dizzy' lady called Linda. I said to her: "Hi Linda. Let me introduce you to Frank."

She looked at him without a flicker of recognition

and replied: "Hello Frank. Do you work with Tony, then ?

She must have been the only person in the building, probably the whole country, who didn't seem to know who on earth the giant, amiable black man in front of her really was.

But even Frank Bruno's larger than life personality did not compare to that of Muhammad Ali, who was the greatest and most charismatic star I ever interviewed.

That happened in August, 1966 after he had come to England to defend his World Heavyweight Championship against Brian London, who he knocked out in the third round at Earl's Court Exhibition Hall.

London liked to 'boss' his opponents, but he seemed apprehensive against Ali, whose speed of punching was truly amazing.

As you may recall, Ali would dance away from his opponents and catch them with his lightening fast long left hand. So London was forced to go reluctantly forward, but with the air of a very cautious man who maybe felt it would be better to back away. Not surprisingly, Ali soon put him out of his misery.

Ali 'entertained' the Press afterwards and I was among those who got to meet the great man - a privilege denied to hundreds of fans milling around the hall.

One of them was an attractive brunette in the

shortest of mini shirts which showed off her amazingly long and shapely legs.

A security man saw me looking at her and said to me: "She's really something, isn't she? She has just given me this envelope to pass on to Ali."

He had already checked its contents, apparently. Now, he opened it completely and there inside was a nude photo of the brunette, dangling her panties tantalisingly from her forefinger, with her phone number scrawled on the back!

We looked across at her and at least she had the decency to blush!

The security man added: "She's wasting her time. Even if I had the nerve to give the photo to Ali, there's no way I'd be stupid enough to do so with all you Press guys around and the TV cameras recording everything!"

The cameras had certainly picked up London's discomfort as he was out-classed and out-fought. He was later to admit that he decided to quit in the third round because he didn't want to risk ending up punch-drunk. London said: "I got paid the same for three rounds as I would have for fifteen." He also admitted: "I always had a go in my fights, but against Ali I didn't try which was totally wrong."

I asked Ali why he was so boastful - was it merely to hype up fights against lesser lights like London or was it to unnerve his opponents? He replied, with a grin: "It's hard to be humble when you're as great as I am."

Despite his total arrogance and brashness, Ali had me and most of the other normally cynical journalists eating out of his hand with his wit, charm, charisma and sheer magnetism.

Ali, previously known as Cassius Clay, had changed his name in 1964 immediately after taking the title, against all the odds, from the ferocious Sonny Liston.

His title shot had almost been ruined when he fought Britain's Henry Cooper at Wembley in 1963. An over-confident Clay was caught by Henry's hammer in a sensational fourth round and seemed to be heading for defeat, but his corner man Angelo Dundee bought him more time to recover between rounds by deliberately enlarging a split in his glove.

Contrary to popular belief, Dundee did not split the glove with a razor. A small tear in the glove had occurred earlier - what the quick-thinking Dundee did was to put his finger into it and make it far worse.

By the time Dundee's demands for a new glove had been sorted out, Clay had recovered and avoided the defeat which might have wrecked all his big money world title plans.

Dundee had already violated the British boxing rules by appearing to use smelling salts to revive Clay in his corner.

The fifth round saw Cassius take full advantage of his let off. He unleashed a lightening fast right hand punch which opened a severe cut under Cooper's eye, causing referee Tommy Little to stop the fight.

Clay confided afterwards: "Cooper's left hand so nearly knocked me out. He hit me so hard that my ancestors in Africa felt it. If the bell hadn't sounded for the end of the round immediately after I got up, then he could have finished the job."

But Cooper felt he would have nailed his man with that one punch if the ropes had not intervened. He revealed: "Unfortunately, the ropes cushioned his fall. If I had hit him away from the ropes perhaps he would have been counted out."

In 1966 Cooper met the renamed Ali, now world heavyweight champion, for a second time at Highbury. Accumulated scar tissue around Cooper's eyes made him even more vulnerable than in the previous contest and a serious cut was opened up by Ali's constant jabs, which led to the fight being stopped.

Fans were divided about Ali's prefight boasts of what he would do to opponents and which round he would beat them in.

But it was all hype. As Ali revealed: "The more I boasted, the more the fans got stirred up and the more tickets they bought to see me."

My Press colleagues and I picked up some great quotes from Ali. He proclaimed: "A man who views the world the same at 50 as he did at 20 has wasted 30 years of his life."

Muhammad had me in stitches with his boasts. He claimed: "I'm so fast that last night I turned off the light switch and was in bed before the room was dark."

And he insisted: "My toughest fight was with my first wife."

My friend Harry Higgins can echo that. When Harry divorced his wife the judge told him: "I've heard all the evidence, Mr. Higgins, and I'm going to give Mrs. Higgins £1,000 a month." Harry was shocked but he replied: "That's very nice of you, Your Honour, I'll try to chip in a few bob myself."

CHAPTER FOUR

# WHAT SINATRA EXPECTED FROM SHIRLEY ANNE

I have become friendly with Shirley Anne Field, one of the most glamorous British starlets ever to graduate to full blown super stardom on the big screen.

My wife Heather and I met her briefly after she gave a fascinating talk, accompanied by film clips of her starring movie roles, to an appreciative audience of Friends of the Devonshire Park Theatre members in Eastbourne in December, 2011.

We have exchanged emails since, as well as having a couple of chats on the phone - and I have found her to be a lovely, kind lady.

Shirley Anne spoke frankly with warmth, grace and humour about her private and professional life during her talk in the Congress Suite, Eastbourne and also told a fantastic story about her date with Frank Sinatra.

Ol' Blue Eyes, at the time the biggest star in the world, was obviously expecting more from her than she was prepared to give after he phoned the then 19-year-old starlet and asked her to be his date when he came to London. He inquired if she 'liked to party' and she said she did, not realising what Sinatra meant by that.

Shirley Ann Field poses with Tony and his wife Heather

He introduced her to a host of celebrities, including Mrs Peter Lawford, sister of John F. Kennedy, and Shirley Anne nervously dropped champagne over her twice!

Frank's charm was replaced by anger when photographers burst into a nightclub to picture them because he incorrectly thought the young actress had tipped off the Press.

To discover how Shirley Anne's remarkable night out with a demanding and controlling show business legend ended, you will need to attend one of her fascinating talks. But I can tell you that after a very eventful night she left with her honour intact!

Shirley Anne also described her tough

upbringing in a children's home in Lancashire where they cut off her lovely long hair, with the aid of a pudding basin, and put her in a bath of cold water.

But she survived with a combination of courage, determination and charm - three of the qualities that were to make her a top film star.

Describing her gruelling work schedule when she was trying to make it in the movie world, Shirley Anne recalled: "I was having to wake at 4 am to be at the studios and I was prepared to give up the film industry."

But, from 500 girls who auditioned, she landed the part of a beauty queen to play opposite Sir Laurence Olivier in 'The Entertainer'.

Shirley then starred in 'Saturday Night and Sunday Morning' with Albert Finney and 'Alfie' with Michael Caine. It changed her life, and the girl from Bolton was wined and dined by the likes of Richard Burton as she made the transition from starlet to respected actress.

She is now in demand to give talks about her fascinating life. But she still found time to encourage me with my writing of children's novels, this book and a comedy script.

The thoughtful Shirley Anne sent me a lovely good luck message to be read out at the film premiere of my comedy 'Hacking It', which surprisingly has nothing to do with the telephone hacking that brought down The News Of The

World. In fact, the oddball characters in the zany local newspaper office I created in my play are so inept that they would think it an achievement to dial a telephone number correctly!

Shirley Anne wrote: “To my new friend Tony Flood, wishing you the best of luck with the film premiere of ‘Hacking It’. It is a rather appropriate title in view of the fact that you have recently had your computer hacked into. Hope you and your executive director Alan Baker have every success by turning ‘Hacking It’ into a TV sitcom (with parts for all of us!).

“Thank you for your books I am reading ‘The Secret Potion’ and enjoying it.”

CHAPTER FIVE

# JOAN COLLINS' WORDS SPELT THE END FOR KATE

Joan Collins is a national institution, but the formidable British actress is not everyone's favourite person and I got the clear impression that is the case with Kate O'Mara, who starred with her in 'Dynasty', one of TV's biggest ever soap operas.

It is hardly surprising because when I spoke to Kate recently she revealed to me that Joan's remarks had led to her being axed from the show.

Joan had landed the starring role of the ruthless Alexis Colby in 1981, but the success enjoyed later in the series by fellow brunette Kate, who played Alexis's scheming sister Caress Morrell, may have rankled with her.

Kate recalled: "A 'Dynasty' producer told me that Joan had said she didn't think it was a good idea to have two brunettes as the main characters in the show. It had apparently taken her two years to reach that conclusion.

"The upshot was that my character was swiftly shipped off to Australia and I was no longer in the show. They simply chose not to take up their option to extend my contract beyond two years.

"I don't know whether Joan felt threatened

by me, but it was ironic that some of the best scenes in 'Dynasty' were those between us.

"If my success in 'Dynasty' did make Joan feel insecure, I suppose in some way it was a backhanded compliment to me."

Kate feels that the decision to axe her in 1988 rebounded on Joan. She explained: "Stephanie Beacham came into 'Dynasty' when I departed and she fires from both hips so I think Joan would have been better off continuing to work with me."

Both Joan and Kate are still working in their seventies. Joan has aged remarkably well and has benefited from not having any facial surgery or Botox.

Kate, who I found to be extremely friendly and helpful, has not undergone surgery, either, but has admitted to having used Botox, which I don't think is a good idea and, in my view, rarely seems to do users any favours.

Kate O'Mara with Tony

She said in a previous interview on Metro: "I've tried Botox, but I don't like it because it stops you being able to use your facial muscles, which, as an actress, are essential. But I do have collagen injections.

"I am fortunate in having this bone structure because I've got a tremendously prominent temple. I like to think that it's because I'm so intelligent.

"My teeth are my worst feature. I've hardly got any of my own left. I've got implants in my upper jaw and hardly any in my lower jaw and that is the problem.

"At one point I thought: 'I'm going to have to do a Marlon Brando and stuff some cotton wool in my mouth'."

I have met Kate twice now following her performances at Eastbourne's Devonshire Park Theatre. The first time was in September, 2011 and she seemed tired after the first night of Agatha Christie's 'Murder On Air', in which I felt the characters she played did not give her as much scope as those of Roy Marsden and the talented Heather Wright.

But Ms O'Mara was in her element as a delightfully-snobbish elderly aunt when she appeared in March this year in another Christie play, 'Murder on the Nile', showing perfect timing in delivering some extremely funny 'put-downs'.

Her equally charismatic co-stars, Susie Amy, from TV's 'Footballers Wives', and Denis Lill (Rodney's father-in-law in 'Only Fools and Horses'), were both generous in their praise of her.

Susie said: "Kate is absolutely terrific," while Denis added: "She's a delight to work with - she's reliable, remembers her lines and has bags of energy."

Above: It's great to have Susie Amy looking up to you

Below: Mark Wynter, Tony, Susie and Denis Lill

CHAPTER SIX

# TERRY SCOTT WAS SO DEMANDING

Actors who are loveable couples in television roles, are not always so perfect in real life.
This could be said about Terry Scott who starred with June Whitfield in hit television sitcom 'Terry and June'.
In real life June Whitfield is equally as wonderful as the doting wife she played on screen and, together with Shirley Anne Field, Susan Penhaligon, Linda Gray, Patsy Kensit, Kate O'Mara, Joanne Heywood and Susie Amy, she is one of the most charming lady actress I have come across.
But her screen husband Mr. Scott was apparently not so gracious.
The popular Daniel Hill, who appeared in one episode of 'Terry and June' when not involved in his own hit 'Waiting for God', recalled how Scott was rude to a fellow actor during filming.
Hill said: "Terry was critical of this actor and asked him: 'Is that how you're going to do it? Even when the poor fellow asked for a bit of understanding because he had not worked for some time, he got little sympathy from Scott."
So Daniel, normally one of the kindest guys you

could hope to meet, decided to teach Terry a lesson. He asked Scott if he would show him how to say his own lines - then requested him to do it twice more to wind him up! The script required Hill to berate Scott's character and when he finally delivered the lines himself he gave Scott a real roasting with a word-perfect, aggressive ticking off.

Hill revealed: "I was in a car with June coming back from location and I asked her: 'How do you put up with him?' She told me that she owed Terry a lot for helping her to become an established television star and that they worked well together. As she said, comics are sometimes a different breed."

The talented Hill, who also played June's son in 'Kingdom', which starred Stephen Fry, added: "June is the best. She's never had a day out of work - she's quite extraordinary. She's now in her eighties and still so professional. She knows everyone's lines as well as her own."

When I spoke to June Whitfield recently she agreed that Terry Scott probably scared the daylights out of some people.

June told me: "Terry could be very critical, and his approach to other people was not always the best. He was a perfectionist and expected high standards from others. If actors didn't know their lines or were not on the ball then he got a bit annoyed. So there were a lot of people he did not get on with.

"But if I felt Terry was being too dominant I gave as good as I got and stood up for myself. I remember him telling me that I should play a scene a certain way so I said 'OK' and then did it the same as before. He was happy and told me that was better!"

However, June pointed out that Terry was a loving family man and had several good points as well. She said: "There were times when he was sweet, affable and charming. We worked so well together and I remember him with affection.

"In fact, people used to think we were not only married in 'Terry and June' but in real life as well.

"This happened when we went to Hong Kong to appear in the play 'Bed Full of Foreigners'. Early one morning there was a phone call to Terry's hotel room and his wife Maggie answered it. She said that Terry was still asleep and the caller asked if he was speaking to June Whitfield. 'No', she replied firmly. 'This is his wife, Mrs. Terry Scott'."

June and Terry first appeared together in his TV series 'Scott On'. She recalled: "The producer and Terry were looking for someone to appear with him in a domestic sketch. I was very nervous when I met him as he was a well established star, but he revealed that he had been nervous,

too, and he told the producer 'She'll do'.
"It was the start of what proved to be a long television partnership and we struck up a very good rapport together."

CHAPTER SEVEN

# BEATLE PAUL PEED ON RIVAL'S SHOES

Husband-and-wife stars I have most enjoyed meeting are actors Brian Murphy and Linda Regan, Jeffrey Holland and Judy Buxton and Bachelors star Dec Cluskey and his wife Sandy, a former dancer in a host of shows.

The Bachelors were once one of the biggest singing groups in the world, out-selling the Beatles and the Rolling Stones in both records and at venues.

Ironically, today many people under the age of 25 might not know about the group's two brothers Dec and Con. But in their heyday they were instantly recognisable.

I have had the great pleasure of socialising with Dec and Sandy Cluskey because they live near me in Eastbourne and he kindly helped to judge a writing competition held by the Anderida Writers, of which I am chairman.

Actually, his judging did not do me any favours with my own entry!

The very busy Dec submitted his markings to the competition secretary Harry Pope later than the other two judges, newspaper editor Keith Ridley and freelance editor Jay Dixon. On their marks, my entry would have been in line for first prize, with nine and eight out of ten respectively. It transpired that all I needed from Dec was a seven to win the competition outright or a six to tie for first place. But after deciding to plough his way through more than 30 entries in one day, he gave me a meagre four!

Nevertheless, I love him to bits and he is one of the most charismatic people I know, with a wonderfully friendly, cheerful personality.

I warmly welcomed him to the Anderida awards night and got on tremendously well with him and his charming wife Sandy, who appeared as a dancer with the likes of Morecambe and Wise and Bruce Forsyth.

She told me this very amusing story of how Dec and she went to see a young Forsyth at London nightspot Talk of the Town and were afterwards invited to his dressing room.

Sandy recalled: "When we went into Bruce's dressing room we found it packed with celebrities, including Sammy Davis Junior and Jimmy Tarbuck.

"Bruce spotted us and made his way through the throng of people to greet us. Dec's face lit up with his usual broad smile as he prepared to accept Bruce's greeting, but instead Bruce went straight up to me and said 'Hello Sandy, it's so great to see you again.' "

It was obviously a blow to her husband's ego.

Dec also told me a wonderful story about how he met Paul McCartney when The Bachelors were the biggest group in Britain and The Beatles were just starting to emerge as their main rivals. He recalled: "The Bachelors were playing the Pavilion in Bournemouth, the huge theatre near the sea front, while a new band called The Beatles were appearing in the small cinema opposite.

"I had heard about the frenzy that accompanied them everywhere, but we had never met, even though we had the same tailor, Dougie Millings, the guy who designed, and made, their famous round collared suits. I remember seeing these suits hanging on the rail at his shop in Soho, waiting to be picked up. Dougie asked: *'Have you ever seen anything so crazy? Some nuts from Liverpool have ordered them'*.

"After we finished our rehearsal in the afternoon at The Pavilion I went across the road to have a peek in at what these guys were up to.

"I went in the stage door. All was quiet and dim - not a soul about. I needed the loo and slipped into the backstage john. The stench nearly knocked me over...but when needs must! Backstage can be a murky place - there is definitely no glamour there.

"I was contentedly enjoying that lovely feeling as all the Guinness is emptied out when the door opened. A guy came in and stood beside

me to relieve himself as well.
"We did the looking up to the sky thing that all men do at a urinal...then, as one, we looked at each other. He jumped, recognising me. I jumped, recognising him ... and yes, the famous Sir Paul peed all over my shoes! I've still got them... stains and all!"
Dec adds that George Harrison happened to have the same girlfriend as him. But adds with a grin: "That's a story for another book."
The generous Dec did me an enormous favour by introducing the film premiere of the comedy play I had written, 'Hacking It', when it was shown for the first time at the Winter Garden Theatre, Eastbourne, in January this year.
I actually welcomed the audience and gave Dec a glowing introduction - my stage manner 'impressed' him so much that he promptly took me to the next meeting of Eastbourne Speakers Club to polish it up.
Perhaps to Dec's surprise I won an award on my first visit for the 'Best Topics Speaker of the Night', but he was not too far off the mark when he joked: "Your content was great, but your delivery was rubbish!"
Since then Dec and his fellow Speakers Club members have been helping me to cut down on my 'ums' and 'ers' and stop referring so much to my notes.
Brian Murphy is instantly recognisable from his

television roles in 'George and Mildred' and 'Last of the Summer Wine', while his wife Linda Regan starred in holiday camp sitcom 'Hi-De-Hi' as Yellow-coat April and is now a successful thriller writer.

When I met Brian and Linda in September, 2011 we talked about how the drop-dead gorgeous actress had come to fall for an actor who rarely got cast in romantic roles.

She recalled: "We appeared together as husband and wife on stage in 'Wife Begins at Forty' in Eastbourne. It wasn't love at first sight and, when Brian asked me out a couple of times during the run, I turned him down, making the excuse that I didn't want to get involved with someone who I was working with.

"So I quite expected him to ask me out again when the show came to an end, but he didn't.

"I missed him, so I drove over to see him at a theatre in Stratford where he was rehearsing for a new play. I suggested he took me for a drink some time - he said 'when' and I said 'today'.

"We were married within a year and have since enjoyed nearly 20 years of happiness together."

Brian told me: "I thought Linda wasn't interested in me after she refused to go out with me so I didn't ask her again. But when she turned up out of the blue I realised I was in with a chance."

Jeffrey Holland, who appeared with Linda in 'Hi-De-Hi' as comedian Spike, is patron of Anderida

Writers so I have got to know him and his wife Judy Buxton quite well and they are a lovely couple.

Jeffrey Holland and his wife Judy Buxton renew old acquaintances

They took the trouble to read - and praise - my script for 'Hacking It'. Jeffrey also kindly wrote a very complimentary review about my wife Heather's children's book 'Mousey Mousey and the Witches' Spells', while Judy did likewise with Heather's 'Giant Sticker Monster and Other Children's Stories'. They have given similar encouragement to other Anderida members and can always be relied upon to help if they have time.

I asked Jeffrey to provide an anecdote for this book and he came up with the following gem:

"When my son Sam was born back in 1976, I was happily ensconced in a national tour of the stage musical of 'Dad's Army', with almost all the original TV cast.

"I was playing Private Walker, the black market spiv, having been promoted from the chorus as the actor who took the part in the London run, John Bardon, couldn't do the tour. It was the proudest time of my career to date! I was a member of Captain Mainwaring's Platoon in the Home Guard!

"We were playing at the Richmond Theatre in July, during one of the hottest summers on record, and towards the end of the midweek matinee performance I was called to the phone at the stage door.

"Having just enough time to take the call before the big finale, I rushed downstairs to hear my mother-in-law's voice telling me that my wife had gone into labour! (This was my first wife, Eleanor, not my present wife, Judy).

"Apparently she had gone in for a routine ante-natal check-up and was told that she was having contractions! She hadn't felt a thing until then!

"Well, knowing that her obstetric history was not good and there were certainly some risks ahead, I asked the two boys who understudied the two parts I played in the show to cover for me that night as I was off!

"I dashed to the station to get a train to Coventry

where we lived at that time.

"I got to Eleanor's bedside by 7 pm and the baby wasn't born until 2.30 am! There were, however, a few problems as anticipated so it was as well that I was there to be with her.

"What I hadn't given any thought to, though, was the wrath of Captain Mainwaring, alias Arthur Lowe! My priority had been to be with my wife in a dangerous situation, and not 'the show must go on!'

"When I arrived back at the theatre the following evening, I found a note waiting for me in my pigeon hole saying: 'Mr Lowe would like to see you in his dressing room.' Oh dear!

"Girding my loins, I made my way up to Arthur Lowe's dressing room and knocked politely on the door. 'Come in!' he called.

"So in I went. Arthur was sitting at his dressing table applying a little colour to his moustache. He didn't look at me! You see, being of the old school, he did believe that 'the show must go on!' 'You wanted to see me, Arthur?' I asked.

"He scolded: 'What you did yesterday was very unprofessional. You should have been here for the show! Babies are born all the time! You should have been here!'

"In a sense he was right, of course, but when I explained my reasons for leaving in such a hurry and the need for me to be there, he melted just a little, and I was sent on my way.

"Needless to say, the first flowers to arrive at the bedside the following day were from the Lowes!"

CHAPTER EIGHT

# OLIVIER'S CUTTING WIT

My great friend Alan G. Baker, a highly respected theatre director, first made his name as a very young actor in the West End, starring as the 'Winslow Boy' at the Haymarket Theatre in the 1950's.

He worked with Sir Laurence Olivier and also has some great stories to tell about Sir Ralph Richardson and Sir John Gielgud.

Alan was treated to a slice of Olivier's cutting wit after his first nervous appearance before the great man as a new member of the Old Vic Theatre cast in 1958.

Baker, then aged 21, was taking a cigarette break during the first read through for 'Richard III'.

He recalled: "I was smoking Guards at the time and Olivier crossed the green room to speak to me. He saw what I was smoking and pulled a packet of Oliviers, named after him, from his pocket. 'Why do you smoke those?' he asked. 'I get coupons with them', I stuttered in reply. 'Ah', he said. 'You get acting parts with these'."

Alan, who in recent years has acted and directed in local theatre productions, mainly with the Seaford Little Theatre, also told me a very amusing tale about Sir Ralph Richardson when he was on stage with him.

He said: "Richardson was quite elderly and on one occasion 'dried' completely. So he walked to the prompt corner because he could not hear properly the cue that was given.

"After listening to the prompt a couple of times, Richardson finally heard his line and walked to the footlights to tell the audience 'very useful chap that, you know'. He got a round of applause."

Alan also told me a great story about Sir John Gielgud getting caught out by his forgetfulness.

He explained: "Gielgud was having a meal with an actor in a restaurant when another actor walked in. Sir John said 'There's that awful fellow .....' but because his memory was so bad he actually named the actor he was sitting with. Seeing the look on the face of his companion, Sir John realised he had insulted him, so he quickly added: "Not you, dear chap - another actor with the same name as you!"

Then there was the story of Noel Coward walking in Leicester Square when he saw a big billboard proclaiming 'Dirk Bogarde and Michael Redgrave - 'The Sea Shall Not Have Them'. His alleged reaction was: 'I don't see why not - everyone else has.' Could he simply have been referring to the fact that fans fantasized about Bogarde and Redgrave so much?

My favourite story of Alan's concerns Dame Edith Evans and her visit to Harrods Store in

Knightsbridge.

It should be remembered that when emphasising a point she would adopt a very high pitched voice as she had done in 'The Importance of Being Ernest' by going up a few decibels upon saying her famous line "handbags!" causing the sound system to blow in rehearsals!

During the war Edith was told that Harrods had received a consignment of pineapples so she went into the store to buy one.

The girl in the fruit department told her that would cost ten shillings and six pence. Edith, feeling this was excessively expensive, repeated in the top range of her voice "Ten shillings and six pence - here is eleven shillings, I think I trod on a grape on the way in."

Alan Baker, who has also directed films, explained to me how the screen was kind to some actors and unkind to others.

He said: "The cameras loved Richard Burton and Elizabeth Taylor who had such well balanced faces. But that brilliant actress Flora Robson did not come across well on screen and was better on stage from a distance. Close up shots of some actors and actresses could portray a face that only a mother would love or age them considerably.

"Gielgud was one of those who looked older on screen - the camera would put up to 20 years on him!"

Alan was the executive director of my comedy 'Hacking It', which was filmed by movie makers Alan Tutt and Harry Lederman, the chairman of The Friends of the Devonshire Park Theatre.
But, despite my best efforts to write him into the play, the exuberant Mr. Baker could not be persuaded to appear before the cameras, and instead devoted his time to coaxing actors from Seaford Little Theatre and Eastbourne Underground Group to play the off-the-wall characters I had dreamed up.
"It's best to concentrate on one job," he remarked.

CHAPTER NINE

# I DIDN'T FIND ABI TITMUSS VERY SEXY

The most disappointing sex symbol I've met has been Abi Titmuss.

Don't get me wrong. I found Abi to be very pleasant to talk to, with no 'side' to her and she is far from being a dumb blonde, but I was expecting a drop dead gorgeous sex-on-legs glamour puss and she did not quite live up to my preconceived notions of her.

Many men have a 'thing' about Abi and have probably drooled over pin-up pictures of the nurse-turned-actress who has teased and tantalized by showing off her 36D-28-34 figure in revealing lingerie, but, in casual clothes and without full make-up, she didn't strike me as THAT sexy.

However, we had a lovely chat in the bar of the Devonshire Park Theatre after she had appeared there in September, 2010 in John Godber's 25th anniversary production of 'Up 'n' Under' involving a woman fitness instructor training a bunch of misfits for a men's rugby league match (despite the title it wasn't the raunchy type of role some theatre-goers might have expected).

Ironically, my friend Colin Dudley, who clearly

Tony was more impressed with Abi's mind

thought Abi was sexy, could not avoid staring at her rather ample boobs, even though they were well covered. And he went bright red when a female member of the group standing around her said: "You can give her a stroke if you want to."

It was some seconds before my friend realised that the lady was referring to Abi's little dog, who had accompanied her to the theatre!

My previous visualization of Abi had resulted from the story of the home-made sex tape that was shot with her former boyfriend and TV presenter John Leslie.

She loyally stood by Leslie when he set out to clear his name of rape allegations concerning

TV presenter Ulrika Jonsson.
When I met Abi she was 35 years old and had made the transition from pin-up girl to serious actress, having won a Best West End Debut award for her performance as a prostitute in Arthur Miller's 'Two Way Mirror'. So she deserves full credit for that.
TV personality Carol Vorderman certainly lived up to my expectations when I bumped into her at a party held in honour of the late Malcolm Richards, my former editor at the Richmond and Twickenham Times.
At the age of 50, Carol won the 'Rear of the Year' award in June, 2011, beating younger candidates like internet sensation Pippa Middleton. But some journalists have suggested that her bottom is now too big to wear figure-hugging dresses.
Carol may not be the same shape as when I was introduced to her, but I reckon that lots of women would love to look like her in their fifties.
Another 'more mature' female celebrity who impressed me with her looks and charisma was American singer-actress Cher, who I encountered in unusual circumstances at London Docklands. I found her to be as staggeringly attractive and engaging in real life as she is on the screen.
I briefly met Cher when she made a personal appearance at an informal function held in

the Docklands by St. Mungo's, a charity which provides help and facilities for the homeless and unemployed.

She found herself surrounded by a big group of homeless people in the reception area and offered words of encouragement by telling them: "If you really want something you can usually figure out how to make it happen."

Quick as a flash, one unshaven, rather scruffy bloke replied: "Does that include having dinner with you at your hotel tonight?"

Patsy Kensit and Erin Boag (both before and after she acquired her new look) also lived up to my expectations of them, while my wife Heather was bowled over by Erin's dance partner Anton du Beke.

When we chatted to him and Erin backstage the charming Anton took Heather's hand and kissed it twice. He then gave her kisses on both cheeks when we said our good-byes.

You can see by the smile how Anton charmed Heather

One 'glamour girl' I turned down the chance to meet was 'X Factor' judge Cheryl Cole.

I just don't like the way this opinionated Geordie and her money-conscious ex-husband, Chelsea footballer Ashley, have come across in certain situations.

England's left-back, nicknamed 'Cashley' by many fans, angered his old club Arsenal and their supporters over a clandestine meeting with London rivals Chelsea while he was still with the Gunners.

He got more bad Press over allegations that he cheated on his wife. Cheryl and Ashley were divorced in September, 2010 after four years of marriage. The decree nisi was granted on the grounds of Ashley's admitted unreasonable behaviour.

The couple had separated seven months earlier following claims in the Press about the England and Chelsea defender's infidelity.

Cheryl had also hit the headlines for the wrong reasons long before her marriage. The Girls Aloud singer, then known as Cheryl Tweedy, was found guilty of assaulting a Guildford nightclub toilet attendant in 2003.

The pop star was sentenced to complete 120 hours of unpaid community service and pay her victim £500 compensation as well as £3,000 for prosecution costs. The singer had denied attacking attendant Sophie Amogbokpa,

claiming she only punched her in self-defence.
In more recent years Cheryl swapped roles and become a judge - on 'X Factor'. Several of her views and decisions on the TV talent show didn't impress me.
I could not see the justice in Cheryl throwing out viewers' favourite singer Gamu Nhengu so that she could put through to the 2010 finals two less charming girls, Katie Waissel and Cher Lloyd, who fluffed the songs they sang at the mentor's house stage of the competition!
Thousands of fans protested, but Cheryl, given the chance to redeem herself when told she could add a 'wild card' to her choices, promptly ignored the talented Zimbabwe teenager again!
I wonder if Cheryl and Ashley Cole will ever fully learn from their mistakes.

CHAPTER TEN

# HOW I HANDLED BOBBY MOORE

Bobby Moore is a soccer legend who proved himself to be a master at reading the game and making snap decisions when captaining England to their only World Cup triumph in 1966.

But when I worked with him I found that he sometimes wasn't the best at making decisions in everyday life!

I had been appointed Head of Sport at controversial tabloid Sunday Sport, with Bobby being given the title of Sports Editor, though the running of the operation was left to me. His duties included covering matches and writing a weekly column, but when asked to express his opinion on an issue Bobby often sat on the fence.

Sunday Sport's abrasive style was to come down heavily on one side of any argument, but Mr. Nice Guy Bobby would at times frustrate us, even when he seemed to offer a firm opinion, by then saying "But on the other hand..." and giving the opposite view.

So I would patiently go through every aspect with him and count up how many 'pros' and 'cons' he came up with. Whatever was the highest would be printed in the paper as his rock solid opinion, with the other side of the coin ignored - and he accepted that.

Bobby remained a sporting icon and was still highly respected throughout the world. One day we received a letter in the office from Brazil, asking Bobby to play in a friendly involving veteran former soccer stars.

He told me he was not available, but asked if I would tell the Brazilians that two other members of England's World Cup winning side, his old West Ham team-mates Geoff Hurst and Martin Peters, probably would be.

I informed the Brazilian FA about this, but the message came back that they only wanted Bobby Moore. Even Hurst, our hat-trick hero against the Germans in that glorious World Cup final, was not considered to be in the same class as Mooro!

Of course, the Brazilians still remembered how well Moore had performed against them in the 1970 World Cup, in which their star player Pele showed his respect for our captain by swapping shirts with him after helping Brazil to beat the holders 1-0.

Pele declared: "Of the hundreds of defenders who played against me during my career I pick Bobby Moore as the greatest of them all. He was also the fairest defender I ever played against."

Bobby returned the compliment. He told me: "Pele was the most complete player I've ever played against or ever seen. He was a great goal scorer and had amazing all-round skill plus a superb footballing brain."

So when they faced each other on the field a fantastic battle of wits resulted because Moore was the most cultured of defenders, clinical in the tackle and strong in the air. He lacked pace, but read the game so well this was seldom a noticeable weakness.

Despite his great successes, Bobby's family have experienced more bad fortune than good.

His first marriage to Tina ended in divorce and she and his second wife Stephanie suffered an even more shattering blow with Bobby's death from cancer, aged 51, in 1993.

Tragedy struck again when Tina and Bobby's son Dean, who worked with Bobby and I at Sunday Sport as a youngster, died in July, 2011, at the age of 43.

Dean, a popular and friendly member of staff while at the paper, was a diabetic. He died after collapsing from a life-threatening complication of the disease, an inquest heard.

His body was found lying on the living room floor at his Notting Hill support centre by a care worker after his worried mother Tina had been unable to contact him.

Next to him were inhalers, a packet of pain-killers and a 'significant amount' of medication including insulin and insulin-delivery systems. Dean, a chef, had a history of alcohol dependency, diabetes, depression, gout and asthma.

His death meant the Moore family had lost a father, son, brother and uncle.

Bobby himself had his share of ill luck. It was in the build up to the 1970 World Cup that the England skipper was involved in one of the game's most controversial incidents.

Moore was accused of stealing a bracelet from a hotel shop in Bogota, Colombia.

A young assistant claimed that he had taken the bracelet without paying for it while accompanying Bobby Charlton in looking for a gift for Charlton's wife, Norma.

This sensational story continued to hog all the headlines as Moore was arrested and then released, but, after helping England win 2-0 against Ecuador, he was placed under house arrest on returning to Colombia.

Diplomatic pressure, plus the fact there was no evidence against Moore, eventually saw the case dropped in time for him to play in the World Cup in Mexico.

No doubt 1970 was Bobby's worst ever year because on August 10th he received an anonymous threat to kidnap his wife and hold her to a £10,000 ransom. This caused him to pull out of two pre-season friendlies

The West Ham legend liked a drink and this got him into trouble the following year. On January 7, 1971, he and three of his Hammers team-mates,

Jimmy Greaves, Clyde Best and Brian Dear, were all fined by West Ham manager Ron Greenwood after going out drinking in a nightclub until the early hours of the morning prior to an FA Cup third round tie against bottom-of-the-table Blackpool, which they lost 4-0.

Moore had been voted the Player of Players when leading England to triumph in the 1966 World Cup, yet he almost missed out on what was to be his greatest triumph. Earlier that year he had seemed set to leave West Ham and let his contract expire.

It was pointed out that Moore would be ineligible to play in the World Cup because he was technically without a club. So England boss Sir Alf Ramsey called upon Greenwood to come to England's training camp at Hendon Hall and give Moore a one-month temporary contract with West Ham to cover the tournament. This allowed Bobby to lead England to glory.

But it appeared that Ramsey seriously considered leaving Moore out of the final.

The England manager had been overheard talking to his coaching staff about the possibility of dropping his skipper and using the more physical and mobile Norman Hunter in preference against the speedy German forwards. Fortunately, he stuck with his captain.

Appropriately, it was Moore's 40-yard perfect pass that set Hurst up for his hat-trick and

England's fourth goal.

Moore opened doors for us at Sunday Sport, as was demonstrated when I put together an All Star team to play in charity matches. The fact he was captaining our Sunday Sport side meant I could persuade the likes of Emlyn Hughes, Malcolm Macdonald, George Graham and John Greig to play.

Tony gets the girl as the stars look on...
Can you spot them? George Graham, Bobby Moore, Frank McLintock, Terry Naylor and the others?

CHAPTER ELEVEN

# DALGLISH RANG ME TO HAVE A RANT

Bobby Moore was so loved that people would go out of their way to please him.

But Bobby was reluctant to ask any favours and he did not call one in from Kenny Dalglish in order to help our chief sports writer Hugh Southern at Sunday Sport as Hugh sought unsuccessfully to get an interview with the Liverpool manager.

This was back in 1988 and we were putting together previews for that year's FA Cup final in which Wimbledon, rank outsiders at 33-1 before the third round in January, turned the form book upside down to reach the final against strongly fancied Liverpool.

I had already interviewed two of the Liverpool players, and passed that story on to our sister paper the Daily Star, so I decided that, for our own Sunday Sport previews, I would chat to some of the Wimbledon players, and Hugh should get some quotes from Liverpool manager Dalglish.

Hugh, skilled at coming up with good story lines, experienced some difficulty in getting hold of King Kenny, and at an office conference Editor Drew Robertson, whose predecessor Mike Gabbert had departed to become Editor of the

Daily Star, wanted the interview done pronto!
Drew said Hugh should leave for Liverpool immediately and present himself at the training ground to ask to see Dalglish. I pointed out that there was little chance that Kenny would give Hugh a lengthy interview without prior arrangement, so Drew turned to Bobby Moore and asked his opinion.
To my surprise, Moore said it was worth giving it a try - so Southern was dispatched forthwith.
He phoned me later from Liverpool to report that he had been to Anfield and was informed it was not possible for him to see Dalglish. I told him that he would need to stay overnight and try again the next day.
Hugh pointed out that he did not have sufficient money with him, or a credit card, to enable him to stay in the Holiday Inn or a similar hotel. It was left to me to explain that the type of low budget accommodation Drew Robertson had in mind for him would not cost him anywhere near as much as the Holiday Inn!
The next day the unfortunate Hugh was again on the phone, telling me he had been to the training ground pleading to see Dalglish, but again without success. He had been reduced to sleeping in his underwear the previous night and was now soaked to the skin so I told him to return.
Ironically, one day later Dalglish phoned the

office, and Hugh answered the phone to him. He must have thought his prayers had been answered until the Liverpool manager told him in a stern voice that he wanted to speak to me. Kenny was not phoning to give Hugh an interview, but to complain that the story I had previously written, quoting two of his players, had appeared in the Daily Star.

He had presumably not realised the Star was our sister paper at that time, which was why I had agreed to let them print my quotes piece.

Dalglish was aggrieved because the Liverpool players' pool had not asked for a fee for the interviews as they knew Sunday Sport had a very small budget. They would presumably have insisted on a payment from the bigger Daily Star to swell the players' FA Cup kitty.

I was dumbfounded at the thought of the great Kenny Dalglish finding time to ring me to complain about the players' pool missing out on a few hundred pounds when he and his squad were earning countless thousands. But perhaps this was just another example of King Kenny sticking up for his players and looking after their interests.

The funny thing about Dalglish in those days was when he was asked any awkward questions by journalists he would often tend to answer in a broad Scottish accent that I found hard to make out. But in his complaint to me he spoke so clearly I could understand every single word! Bobby Moore thought the whole thing was greatly amusing, and I believe even Hugh saw the funny side after securing a telephone interview with Liverpool legend Tommy Smith on how the final would go.

Of course, Tommy and almost everyone else were wrong with their predictions, because, against all odds, little Wimbledon beat the mighty Merseysiders 1-0.

Talking about getting things wrong, I am not alone in feeling that, while Dalglish deserves credit for reviving Liverpool in his second spell as their manager, he has made mistakes when it comes to public relations, particularly in his handling of the Luis Suarez affair.

Dalglish surprised me by backing an inappropriate decision that his players wear T-shirts in support of Suarez and claiming that the provocative Uruguayan striker should not have been suspended for eight games by the FA for racially abusing Manchester United's Patrice Evra.

But then Kenny really shocked me with his reaction after Suarez marred his first start following his return by refusing to shake hands with Evra as the teams lined up for another match against United in February this year.

The Liverpool manager, interviewed by Sky TV after the explosive 2-1 defeat by United, said he had been unaware that Suarez had snubbed Evra.

Sky reporter Geoff Shreeves informed him firmly, but politely, that Suarez had, in fact, refused to shake Evra's hand.

Shreeves was scowled at by the dour Scot, who told him: "I think you are bang out of order to blame Luis Suarez for anything that happened out there." Dalglish refused to even criticise his player's conduct.

It was in stark contrast to the reaction of United boss Sir Alex Ferguson, who called for Suarez to be booted out of Anfield.

Sir Alex raged: "I just could not believe it. That player should not be allowed to play for Liverpool again. It could have caused a riot."

It was not until a day later that Dalglish and Liverpool seemed to fully realise the damage this had done to the club. They were then anxious to correct what had been a public relations disaster.

Suarez issued a statement of apology at 2.16 pm, followed by others from Liverpool chief executive Ian Ayre at 2.30 pm and Dalglish at 3.30 pm.

Dalglish's statement said: "Ian Ayre has made the club's position absolutely clear and it is right that Luis Suarez has now apologised for what happened at Old Trafford.

"To be honest, I was shocked to hear that the

player had not shaken hands, having been told earlier in the week that he would do so.

"But, as Ian said earlier, all of us have a responsibility to represent this club in a fit and proper manner and that applies equally to me as Liverpool manager.

"When I went on TV after yesterday's game I hadn't seen what had happened, but I did not conduct myself in a way befitting of a Liverpool manager during that interview and I'd like to apologise for that."

Managers should learn that if they are dismissive of questions asked them by reporters, they are usually failing to give their own supporters the information they are seeking.

It's the same with politicians. When David Cameron insults Ed Miliband (and vice versa) in the House of Commons they are scoring cheap points while refusing to provide answers that we (the voters) want to know!

Hopefully, Dalglish has learned a lesson in public relations. It would be great if Messrs Cameron and Miliband also improved their knowledge of public perceptions and their manners at Prime Minister's Question Time!

One thing they could learn from King Kenny is how to motivate and inspire their teams, which he does so well!

Dalglish also rides his luck at times, as he did when Liverpool pipped gallant Cardiff 3-2 in a nerve-racking penalty shoot-out at the end of the Carling Cup final in February this year after being held to a 2-2 draw following extra-time. But he deserves full credit for ending Liverpool's six-year wait for a trophy by fielding his strongest team in a competition which many other managers under-value.

Those managers who went out in earlier rounds after selecting teams full of reserves were surely misguided. They presumably felt they were justified in saving their key players for the league games ahead, but they were passing up a chance of glory for everyone at their club.

Dalglish's former Scotland manager Tommy Docherty agrees. He told me: "Kenny was rewarded for fielding his strongest side. I believe that managers who don't do that are cheating their supporters and belittling the competition.

"It has backfired on them because if they had fielded their best team in every round they might have made it to the final - winning the Carling Cup would have been great to have on their CV and a real boost for their club."

The downside came when Liverpool suffered a dreadful run in the league and Dalglish blamed it on them being tired from their cup exertions, but the Reds slide raised question marks about his future.

Of the row over Suarez, one-time Manchester United boss Docherty commented: "It did not surprise me that Kenny supported his player - he has always been loyal to his players.

"And I think Ferguson was out of order in saying that Suarez should not have been allowed to play for Liverpool again. In my view Sir Alex was not entitled to tell Liverpool how to run their club.

"But I am biased because I am a friend of Kenny Dalglish. I gave him his first 15 caps for Scotland in the 1970's. Jock Stein, the former Scotland manager, told me I was wrong to pick him because Kenny wasn't ready, but he was the best player in our team, a different class to the rest."

CHAPTER TWELVE

# PETER SELLERS MADE WIFE BRITT SQUIRM

When I interviewed actress Britt Ekland I found her to be guarded about what she would say, especially concerning her former husband Peter Sellers.

But she did not deny he was obsessive, and this applied to his relationship with members of the Royal family.

The former Hollywood actress, who probably had better things to do than be interviewed by me for her forthcoming appearance in a local theatre production, could not be coaxed into saying much more on the subject.

However, her revelation that: "I'd squirm with embarrassment at the lengths he (Sellers) would go to in order to ingratiate himself with the Royal family," speaks volumes.

In her autobiography 'True Britt' she revealed: "I was completely unaware of his connection with the British monarchy. One afternoon before we married he had disappeared, saying that he had to do something 'important'.

"I was to learn he had spent the afternoon having tea with the Queen Mother at Clarence House."

Sellers was a close friend of Princess Margaret

and she appeared in one of his home movies.

Britt, who in her prime was one of the world's most beautiful women, told me she did not approve of the biopic about Sellers. She stressed: "It bore no relationship to real life whatsoever. Nobody bothered to ask me what life with Peter Sellers was like.

"I could have told them so much. I still have all my diaries, photos and letters Peter and I exchanged."

My 20 minute chat with Britt in 2005 was to preview her forthcoming appearance on stage in the comedy 'Just Desserts!' at Richmond Theatre - a long way from the height of her Hollywood career in which she starred in two films with Sellers before divorcing him.

But the stylish Swede insisted: "I don't miss the Hollywood lifestyle - I'm still leading a hectic life and work nine months of the year. I simply keep fit by walking my dog and doing stretches. The reason I still look good is down to genetics."

At the then age of 62, she was no doubt less under the publicity spotlight than in her heyday when her romances with Rod Stewart and Warren Beatty hit the headlines.

Britt, who described Beatty as "the most divine lover of all with a libido that was as lethal as high octane gas," told me that modern actors lacked the charisma of former Hollywood greats.

She said: "When I was at the height of my career

in the 1960's, there were some real characters in Hollywood. Now actors lack charisma and stature - leading men like Tom Cruise are on the short side."

One of her career highlights was playing opposite Michael Caine in 'Get Carter'. Asked about the remake, she commented: "I haven't seen it and wouldn't want to. What makes Sylvester Stallone think that he has the sensitivity to do what Michael Caine did?

"Unfortunately, some of the giants of the screen can never be replaced."

But fellow actress Patsy Kensit disagreed. She insisted to me: "There are still some very big personalities around such as Hugh Grant and George Clooney."

My interview with Patsy at the Richmond Theatre underlines why it does not always pay for a journalist to be completely up-front or to underestimate the opposition.

Just before fellow journalist Catherine Usher and I did a joint interview with Miss Kensit for two local papers, Catherine showed me an article in a tabloid in which Patsy had talked openly about her love life.

But Catherine left it to me to ask Patsy to confirm that her first three husbands had been the true loves of her life. Patsy replied that she did not want to talk about her private life, which seemed slightly hypocritical seeing that she had told all to the national paper.

As a result of my tame and perfectly legitimate question, the Press Officer who was accompanying Patsy asked me to let her see my story before it was published in the Richmond and Twickenham Times Series so that she could have the right to approve it.

I refused, saying that Patsy had not been offended by the question in any way, as she had proved by posing for pictures with me and even running her hand across my chest to make the pictures look more intimate. But I said I would not include anything about her love life in my story.

The female Press Officer did not ask the innocent looking Catherine if she could see her story before it went into print. So she must have been shocked, as I was, when Cathy lifted Patsy's most revealing quotes from the tabloid paper exclusive, as well as from other cuttings, disclosing in her story extensive details about the loves of Miss Kensit's life!

Even so, there have been other relationships which Cathy did not mention - those allegedly with Ally McCoist, Calum Best, David Walliams, Matt Holbrook, Jean-Christophe Novelli and beatboxer Killa Kela.

Kensit later became involved with DJ Jeremy Healy and announced that she was marrying for a fourth time in November, 2007. Within four months it was claimed that the pair had called off their wedding. They eventually married on April 18, 2009, but the Daily Mail reported in February, 2010 that the couple had separated.

Kensit vowed never to marry again following this split, describing it as “embarrassing and humiliating.”

Surely it could not have been as humiliating as being dumped by married footballer Ally McCoist after discovering that she had not been his only mistress.

Patsy had turned to McCoist following her marriage break-up with Liam Gallagher, which had caused her to say: “I’m so happy that all the mess I used to have to deal with is not my mess any more.”

Unfortunately, there was a lot more mess in store for her. Patsy apparently did not deny she was having an affair with McCoist, and when it was reported in the Press in September, 2001 she may have felt this would cause him to leave his wife.

Instead, it came out that he had also been having an affair with 28-year-old air hostess Donna Gilbin. And to complete Kensit’s embarrassment, McCoist promptly ended their relationship.

Poor Patsy has had it tough most of her life. Her father was not the antiques dealer she’d been led to believe, but had gangland connections and a criminal record. James ‘Jimmy The Dip’

Kensit was an associate of the notorious London gangsters the Kray twins and the Richardsons and he served time in prison before she was born.

Goodness knows what that Press Officer would have said if Cathy or I had brought any of this up at our interview!

Patsy, a gritty English girl from Hounslow, Middlesex, had starred with some of the biggest actors in the world, having played opposite Mel Gibson in 'Lethal Weapon 2' and Anthony Hopkins in 'A Chorus of Disapproval'. Yet she admitted to me that sharing the Richmond stage in 'Aladdin' with highly respected Shakespearean actor Simon Callow was rather daunting.

She said: "I was in awe of Simon and it took me ages to make eye contact with him."

As she was performing in a low cut pantomime costume, it may have been equally hard for him to make eye contact with her! After all, she had a breast augmentation which took her bust measurement from a 32B to a 35C.

Another actress who made a big impression on me was Linda Gray, the star of TV soap opera 'Dallas'.

We had a most enjoyable chat after one of her stage performances and I found her to be most friendly.

Linda revealed that originally she was given only a small part in the first series of 'Dallas', which was to become one of the most successful ever soaps.

She said: "Larry Hagman and I were so wonderfully evil together, and had so much fun acting off each other, that they beefed up my part.

"In the first episode I wasn't referred to and never as J.R.'s wife." But she loved playing Sue Ellen and told me: "A lot of women could relate to her."

CHAPTER THIRTEEN

# AGE HAS CAUGHT UP WITH PETULA CLARK

Age eventually catches up with all of us including even the most glamorous of stars.

Classic examples of this are singers Mick Jaggar, Tommy Steele and Petula Clark.

When I reviewed one of Petula's stage shows a few years ago she looked as lively and bouncy as ever on stage.

But in my interview with her afterwards I was shocked to see that the physical ageing process had not been kind to her. Fortunately she had lost none of her charm and sparkle.

The singer, actress and composer, who was born 79 years ago on November 15th, 1932, has had an amazing career spanning eight decades during which she has sold more than 68 million records!

She revealed: "At first I didn't want to be a singer, but for a youngster in England during the war there wasn't an awful lot around."

Her father had taken her to see Flora Robson on stage back in 1938 and she said: "I made up my mind I wanted to be an actress I wanted to be Ingrid Bergman more than anything else in the world."

Petula accepts that today's youngsters don't know who she is

I found Petula to be totally realistic when she told me: "Maybe many youngsters don't know who I am because most of them are so engrossed in the current pop scene. I don't find that frustrating - just somewhat amusing.

"The world is constantly changing and longevity cannot be guaranteed. Perhaps Madonna will be the last big star to survive the test of time."

Even those youngsters to whom the name Petula Clark means nothing should recognise Downtown, her smash hit record which topped the US charts and launched her American career 48 years ago.

Some stars still look remarkably good for their age such as Joan Collins, Cliff Richard, Shirley Bassey and Tony Blackburn.

Tony, the winner of the ITV reality programme 'I'm A Celebrity...Get Me Out of Here!' in 2002, was the first disc jockey to broadcast on BBC Radio 1 in 1967.

You would think that a DJ, who had as much success and made as many radio and television appearances as Blackburn did in those days, would be full of confidence - perhaps even slightly arrogant.

But that is not the case. He actually seemed to be the opposite when I rescued him from queueing outside Stringfellows night club where Sunday Sport were holding a celebration party in the late 1980's.

And he even did a runner some 10 years earlier when my friend Clive Hogben yelled out to him in the street because he had left his wallet in Clive's shop.

Clive recalls: "Tony Blackburn came into the shop where I was assistant manager to order a music centre.

"After he had gone I saw that he'd left his wallet behind so I ran out of the shop after him and shouted his name. He did not recognise me, and seeing me running towards him clearly frightened him.

"So Tony ran off down Tottenham Court Road

with me in pursuit. I grabbed him outside the underground station, and he was a very relieved man when I explained that I simply wanted to return his wallet to him."

CHAPTER FOURTEEN

# FRANKIE HOWERD HID THE FACT HE WAS GAY

I have met many comedians, including the great Max Miller, Frankie Howerd, Jimmy Carr, Cannon and Ball, Mike Reid and Jim Tavaré, who gave me backstage access to a charity event he held so that my son James and I could chat to Tim Vine, Lee Mack, Al Murray, Harry Hill. Paul Tonkinson and Frank Skinner.

Doing stand-up can be one of the toughest jobs in show business as I discovered when I tried it myself.

I got the laughs with a Bob Monkhouse-style routine containing loads of wife jokes, but I was terrified I would dry up. And even when I performed to a crowd of 1,000-plus, I didn't have to worry about pleasing a television audience like real comedians do. The prospect used to worry Frankie Howerd so much he was often physically ill with stage fright before a performance.

But the worst thing for comedians these days is when television networks turn their backs on them. Tommy Cannon and Bobby Ball both moaned to me about how they had been largely ignored by TV until they resorted to appearing on the reality show 'I'm A Celebrity...Get Me

Tony with Paul Tonkinson and Frank Skinner

Out Of Here' in 2005.

Cannon and Ball had their differences during their hey-days in the 1980's when they were barely on speaking terms, but have since become very close again.

Bobby revealed: "We ended up falling out. I think it was egos taking over. I thought I was the main one in the act and Tommy thought he was the main one in the act." He paused for effect and joked: "He should have realised it was me."

Tommy explained that the relationship hit rock bottom during a summer season in Bournemouth. He recalled: "Backstage in Bournemouth was a long corridor, with Bobby's dressing room at the bottom end and mine at the top end. We had to turn side by side to pass in the corridor and we wouldn't even speak to each other.

"I used to go home at night and cry - it was one of the worst periods of my life."

They didn't get on for four years, but everything changed when Cannon and Ball met a vicar and both became Christians. Bobby said: "I started seeing the good in Tommy and not the bad. We had hated one another, but now we love each other."

A similar thing happened to Little and Large, which was one of the topics of conversation when I interviewed Syd Little last year.

Eddie Large had revealed in an interview in 2010 that he hadn't spoken to Syd for several years.

Syd claimed: "We would both think up sketches and I used to get frustrated because mine would never get accepted. I felt bullied by Eddie - if I screwed up he'd give me this look. It used to make me worse."

But Eddie, the star of the act in which Syd played the straight man, disagreed. He said: "That's not how I remember it...maybe his ideas were crap ideas. I don't remember him complaining when we were making fortunes.

"Syd was nervous and that made me nervous that he wouldn't remember the lines."

But what brought the act to a sudden end was Eddie's heart problems. He recalled: "I was told I could drop dead at any minute. I had to stop working and have a heart transplant."

Most comedians have had dips in their careers

as was the case with Frankie Howerd, who was haunted for many years by the fear that his fans would discover he was gay. He even paid blackmail demands to conceal it.

He was also paranoid about his hair loss, but when I met him in his dressing room it was obvious he was wearing a wig and there seemed to be a trace of glue at the top of his sideburns. I found him in a good mood and very friendly, but fortunately not over-friendly, as he apparently was on one occasion when he was alone with Bob Monkhouse, who quickly made his excuses and left!

At the time I met him, the so camp Frankie was making a comeback after his career had taken a dive. He was greatly relieved to be able to bounce back due to new satirical material written for him by Ray Galton and Alan Simpson. Galton and Simpson gave me some useful tips when they came round to tea with my wife Heather and I at our house in Twickenham after I had met Alan on various occasions and interviewed Ray. They also told me about the sad demise and suicide of one of Britain's greatest comedians, Tony Hancock, who felt so insecure he was seldom satisfied in his professional or private life and resorted to drink.

Hancock committed suicide on June 25th, 1968 at the age of 44. And Ray Simpson said: "I was not shocked when I was told about it. I had expected it for years it was the only way out for him."

Galton and Simpson compared the careers of former comedians with the likes of Bruce Forsyth and Jimmy Tarbuck, who became overnight successes by hosting 'Sunday Night At The London Palladium'.

Ray Galton and Alan Simpson came to tea

It was back in 1958 when Forsyth was appearing at the Royal Hippodrome in Eastbourne that impresario Val Parnell booked him to compère 'Sunday Night at the Palladium'. But Forsyth showed no gratitude to the Hippodrome. He recalled in the television programme '100 Years of the Palladium': "I got the call from Val when I was working in this terrible theatre at Eastbourne with a cast of 10 and an orchestra of two pianos and drums. I went from that to a 30-piece orchestra as host at the Palladium - the biggest job on television."

Bruce revealed: "Suddenly restaurants were giving me meals on the house. Previously when I was starving for a meal they didn't even offer me a loaf of bread and some water."

Other comedians tell jokes about Forsyth's ego. My favourite is when Bruce supposedly made a personal appearance at an old people's home. He was in the reception area when an old person asked if she could help him.

Forsyth allegedly replied: "Do you know who I am?" And the old person said: "Ask matron, she'll tell you."

Brucie admits himself that he has an ego, but claims he has changed a lot over the years. He told Jenny Johnston in an interview published in the Daily Mail's Weekend magazine in January this year: "I'm quite shocked myself when I listen to what I sounded like 30 years ago. The pitch is completely different now - everything is much deeper.

"It was a bit camp, wasn't it?... People did think I was gay when I first started...I proved afterwards that I wasn't gay - probably too much in some regards."

Bruce is a TV legend, of course, and few would begrudge him finally receiving in October, 2011, at the ripe old age of 83, the knighthood he had waited for so long after 70 years in show business.

Talking of legends, Max Miller was Britain's top

variety hall comic in the 1930's through to the 1950's and I met him in his last West End show at the Palace Theatre in 1959.

I was just 16 when my grandfather and stepfather treated me to a night out to see The Cheeky Chappie, famous for his flamboyant suits and risqué rapid-fire jokes that often got him into trouble with the censors.

Apparently, Max was less quick to part with his money. This probably accounted for the fact that, after we found him in the bar at the interval and bought him a drink, he did not turn up afterwards to return the favour as he had promised.

Fellow comedian Roy Hudd later revealed that the thrifty Max was not in the habit of buying drinks!

CHAPTER FIFTEEN

# PASQUALE'S TALENT SHOW VOTES SECRET

I had to make do with a telephone interview with comedian Joe Pasquale, but it was an enjoyable experience because he was prepared to answer most of my questions fully and frankly.

One thing he did not talk so freely about was his attempt to swing the voting in his favour while appearing as an unknown on television talent show 'New Faces' in 1987.

His high-pitched voice seemed to go even higher as he admitted that a little help from several hundred new 'friends' put him on the way to stardom.

Joe later made a 'full confession' when appearing on ITV's 'The Talent Show Story' last January - 25 years after the event.

He said: "Before I went on 'New Faces' I was a bingo caller and refereed wrestling at a holiday camp, so I had nothing to lose.

"One of the judges was Ken Dodd and he gave me advice on how to improve my act. I did what he said and won the heat.

"I then needed to win the postcard vote to reach the final. I was still working at a holiday camp where we had about 400 people staying each week. I bought a job lot of 5,000 postcards and dished them out to guests after I had filled them in. All they had to do was stick a stamp on and post them."

Joe gave a sly grin as he added: "Whether they sent them in I don't know, but I got through on the viewers' votes."

In the final, decided by votes being phoned in across the country, Joe was pipped by ventriloquist Jimmy Tamley. They were level on points when the last telephone vote from the Midlands gave Tamley victory.

But Pasquale recalled: "The fact I came second meant I got a wave of sympathy, saying 'you should have won'. I'd rather have 'you were robbed' than people going 'how did you win?'

Joe may act the fool with a succession of visual gags on stage, but he is one shrewd cookie as he proved when increasing his popularity by appearing on - and winning - 'I'm A Celebrity... Get Me Out Of Here!' in 2004.

Talking of visual humour, three of the greatest natural comedians have been Tommy Cooper, Norman Wisdom and Ken Dodd. That view is endorsed by fellow entertainer Chris Stone, a vice president of Clowns International.

He told me: "Norman Wisdom and Ken Dodd have also been vice presidents of Clowns International, which has 300 working clowns as members, and both of them appeared at our festivals.

"When Ken came to our festival in Bognor in 1989 it was his first public appearance after being charged with tax evasion in a court case that lasted three weeks and resulted in him being acquitted.

"We went through the town on an open top bus and Ken was worried about the reception he would get from the public. He told us he feared some of the crowd might boo him. But 100,000 people cheered their heads off as he waved to them - they loved the fact he had got the better of the Inland Revenue."

To really rub it in to the tax man, Ken joked: "When income tax was first introduced it was at a rate of 2p in the pound...I thought it still was!"

Chris added: "Ken and Norman Wisdom have been two of the greatest comics I've come across.

"They, like Tommy Cooper, were blessed with the ability to make people laugh before they even opened their mouths.

"Norman was also a great prankster. I remember when he was due to appear at a Clowns International event in Southport. He came into the Green Room before the show limping and said he wouldn't be able to go on as he was feeling ill.

"We were all very concerned about him as he sat there looking poorly. After all, he was about 70 years old.

"Then suddenly Norman leapt up, did a forward roll and said 'I'm OK now'. He went on to give an hilarious performance."

CHAPTER SIXTEEN

# UNITED COULD HAVE ENDED UP WITH VENABLES

Apart from Bobby Charlton, I also interviewed a lot of other Manchester United icons, such as Pat Crerand, Lou Macari and Gordon McQueen, particularly during my time as Sports Editor of Fleet Street News Agency, which provided stories to all the national papers.

My chats with United manager Sir Alex Ferguson, club chairman Martin Edwards and other insiders at Old Trafford resulted in some very interesting revelations.

This included the fact that United came close to appointing an outspoken, love-him-or-'hate'-him Cockney as their manager in Terry Venables. When Martin Edwards and his fellow directors Charlton, Maurice Watkins and Mike Edelson appointed Ferguson back in November, 1986 as a replacement for Ron Atkinson they also seriously considered Venables for the job.

They were impressed by the fact El Tel had taken Barcelona to the European Cup final that year and had won the Spanish League the previous season.

But Ferguson's great record with Aberdeen made him the No. 1 choice, and only if he had turned United down would Venables have got the job.

Unfortunately, this information was given to me 'off the record' which was a pain in the neck because it meant I was honour bound not to use any of the comments made to me!

During his amazing 25 years in charge of United, Alex Ferguson has proved to be one of the greatest managers in the game. Some journalists will also tell you he has been one of the most intimidating, depending upon what sort of mood he has been in when they have encountered him!

It's as if there are TWO Alex Fergusons. Sometimes he can appear to be a bit of a 'smart Aleck' - confrontational, critical and sarcastic. On other occasions he is very caring and compassionate.

I was fortunate to talk to him two or three times on the phone when he was still finding his feet in his job at Old Trafford back in 1986, and found him to be helpful and informative, which was very good of him, especially as he didn't know me.

But I expect Sir Alex would have been less friendly towards me if I had met him after my comments about him when I made one of my regular appearances as a sports analyst as part of BBC television's 'News 24' in February, 2003. He had injured his own star player David Beckham by angrily kicking a boot across the dressing room, causing it to hit Beckham just above the left eye.

The incident occurred when Ferguson showed his displeasure at losing 2-0 to old rivals Arsenal in the fifth round of the FA Cup.

I was asked what I thought about Ferguson's reaction. I acknowledged that it was an accident, but made it clear that I felt Fergie was out of order in kicking a boot about, and should learn to curb his temper.

Ferguson laughed it off. He said: "It was a freakish incident. If I tried it 100 or a million times it couldn't happen again. If I could do it again I would have carried on playing!"

Some United players deserved to receive Fergie's 'hair-dryer' rollickings far more than Beckham.

Dwight Yorke upset his manager on several occasions, but probably none more so than when he was found to have taken part in a romp with four girls and the then Aston Villa goalkeeper Mark Bosnich.

Yorke secretly videoed the drink-fuelled sexual activities at his luxury house in Sutton Coldfield. The video showed Yorke and Bosnich giving thumbs-ups to the secret camera and wearing women's clothing as a joke.

They would have got away with it had Yorke not thrown the video out in his rubbish bin. Unfortunately for him a 'Sun reader' found it - and when the pictures appeared in print Fergie was understandably furious.

Even a disciplinarian like Ferguson has not been able to prevent other United players being involved in kiss-and-tell encounters.

In recent times the most damaging have been the revelations about Ryan Giggs, who was named in Parliament as the footballer who had taken out an injunction to avoid claims of an affair with Big Brother's Imogen Thomas becoming public.

Giggs is understood to have spent around £200,000 on legal fees trying to keep a lid on the affair.

Ironically, it also came to light that he had an eight-year relationship with his sister-in-law Natasha Giggs.

There was massive Press coverage about it as the 29-year-old Natasha said she was a 'fool' to risk her marriage to the player's brother Rhodri for the thrill of having a relationship with someone as famous and admired as the 38-year-old star.

The 'off-the-record' revelation about Terry Venables being the second choice to Fergie for the United job reminds me of an amusing story when I was Sports Editor of the Lancashire Evening Telegraph and Star in Blackburn at the start of the Eighties.

My main two sports writers Peter White and Keith McNee provided most of our page leads, but we also had an excellent writer in former

Northern Ireland international soccer star Jimmy McIlroy, who had been possibly the greatest player Burnley ever had.

On one occasion Jimmy came up with the best story of the day following his interview with then Blackburn Rovers manager Howard Kendall, and so I told one of my sub-editors to use it as the back page lead.

After a few minutes the sub-editor came up to me and said: "Tony, have you read much of this story?"

"Only the first three paragraphs," I replied. He directed my attention to the fourth paragraph in which McIlroy quoted Kendall as saying: "Completely off the record..."

Jimmy had not appreciated what 'off the record' meant and was disappointed when I told him we were having to ditch his 'exclusive' because Kendall was giving the information only on a 'not-for-publication' basis.

CHAPTER SEVENTEEN

# MATTHEWS HAULED UP OVER SPENDING SIX PENCE

Two of the most charming male personalities I've interviewed were old time footballers Sir Stanley Matthews and Sir Tom Finney.

Stan and Tom were almost certainly the greatest players of their generation and yet they were so natural and modest.

Few of today's multi-millionaire footballers show a similar degree of modesty - two of the exceptions are Chelsea's Frank Lampard and Liverpool's Steven Gerrard, both of whom I also found charming to interview.

Matthews was an even bigger hero than Lampard or Gerrard are today - certainly he

Hall of Fame....
Steven Gerrard, Dave Mackay and Frank McLintock with Tony looking on.

was rated more highly than any of the current stars by his adoring Blackpool fans. Yet he was not given the respect due to him by some of his 'masters' at the Football Association.

I remember Matthews saying that when he travelled to Scotland to play for England at Hampden Park in 1948 he changed trains at Carlisle where he bought a cup of tea for six pence in the station buffet.

He submitted an expense claim for this to the FA and had it rejected by some petty accounts person!

Here was England's top star, who had helped to attract a massive crowd of over 130,000 to Hampden Park, being scolded over charging expenses of far less than £1 in present day values for a cup of tea.

Can you imagine what would happen if the FA did that to one of today's over-paid stars?

Matthews' match fee for helping England beat the Scots was a meagre £14, and he had to travel from Stoke to Glasgow on a second-class rail ticket.

Matthews played his final game at the ripe old age of 50 for Stoke City on February 6$^{th}$, 1965 after seeing out his career on the maximum wage of £20 a week!

The Wizard of Dribble scored 71 goals in 701 league and cup games, but he will always be remembered for his role in helping Blackpool come back from 3-1 down to beat Bolton 4-3 in the 1953 FA Cup final.

Stanley Mortensen scored a hat-trick in that Wembley epic, yet it has always been known as 'The Matthews final.'

I played with Mortensen and some of the other Blackpool players from that team in a charity match years later while on holiday at the seaside town.

When I was brought on as a substitute, the match commentator, comedian Freddie 'Parrot Face' Davies, took one look at my baulky frame and announced: "Now, taking the field wearing two pair of shorts, is Tony Flood."

I found that Mortensen was extremely modest, and was not at all bitter that a final in which he scored three goals should be named after someone else!

Matthews was given a free role in the Blackpool side, partly because of his great skill and partly because manager Joe Smith was not a great one for tactics.

Sir Stanley revealed: "Joe just told us to go out and enjoy ourselves.

"At half-time against Bolton we were losing 2-1, but we remained calm. We simply sipped our tea and listened to Joe. He didn't rant or rave - he just told us to keep playing our normal game."

After Mortensen had levelled the scores, Matthews set up the winner for Bill Perry in the last minute of injury time. He recalled in his autobiography: "Ernie Taylor rounded Langton and found me wide on the right. I took off for what I knew would be one final run to the byline.

"I jinked past Banks and, as Barrass came in, I pulled the ball back to where experience told me Morty would be. In making the cross I slipped on the greasy turf and, as I fell, my heart and hopes fell also.

"I saw that Morty was not where I expected him to be, but had peeled away to the far post. For five years we'd had this understanding. He knew exactly where I'd put the ball. Now, in this game of all games, he wasn't there.

"But Bill Perry raced up from a deep position and coolly stroked the ball wide of Hanson and Ball on the goal-line into the corner of the net."

Matthews was never booked in almost 700 league games spanning 39 years. No modern day player will ever match that record!

CHAPTER EIGHTEEN

# OSGOOD FEARED FOR OLD MANAGER

Perhaps the most fun I had was running a soccer coaching course for youngsters with former Chelsea star Peter Osgood in Tolworth, Surrey.
I organised the course through a local newspaper and it attracted almost 150 young applicants, including my own son James, a rather reluctant recruit as soccer did not really appeal to him.
Osgood and another former Chelsea player, Allan Harris, agreed to take the coaching, and I invited along soccer legend Ted Drake to make a special guest appearance.
Drake had set a club record as a centre-forward with Arsenal by scoring 44 league and cup goals in the 1934-5 season and went on to manage Chelsea, leading them to their first ever championship in 1954-55.
This had happened before the youngsters on our course were born so, of course, they didn't know who he was when they saw this well built elderly man stride over to where we were coaching in groups.
Despite the fact it was raining, Ted was wearing a smart blazer and grey trousers.
One of the kids in my group asked his mate: "Who is this old guy?" I told him that Ted had

been one of the greatest strikers in the game and his neck muscles were so strong he could head a ball harder than anyone.

Drake offered to demonstrate even though he was in his eighties.

I threw the ball in the air to Ted and he headed it at the young lad so hard that it knocked him over.

The kids loved it and Ted was asked to repeat the trick but as he did so Peter Osgood came running across shouting: "Tony, what are you doing - you'll kill him!"

I also arranged and played in a few charity football matches, including one for Bobby Moore's Sunday Sport XI against Osgood and a Chelsea Old Stars XI.

In the opening minutes Bill Garner of the Chelsea Old Stars looked like breaking through until Emily Hughes, the former Liverpool star, intervened.

But I then saw a Chelsea boot appear to go over the top of the ball, and Hughes went down with his leg bleeding from stud marks.

It was serious enough for Hughes to be taken to hospital. Such incidents were unheard of in a charity match.

Afterwards I asked Osgood what it was all about. He told me that when they were playing League Football Hughes had got the Chelsea man sent off.

"How long ago was that?" I asked.
Osgood replied: "Oh, about 15 years!"
Such is the tough mentality of many professional footballers - as I found out again when I organised a match for the Ferry Disaster Fund in which Malcolm Macdonald bravely agreed to play to help raise money for the cause despite being almost crippled with arthritis in his knees. Supermac, famed for scoring goals for Luton Town, Newcastle United, Arsenal and England, could barely run, but the opposition showed little sympathy. They hardly allowed him a kick, It didn't seem to occur to them that the crowd were desperate to see a glimpse of Malcolm's once lethal shooting.
I had the privilege of playing up front with McDonald in an All Star XI against a team of former Charlton and Gillingham players. I was only due to come on as a substitute, but George Graham kindly told me to go on in his place for the first-half.
I arranged a couple of other all star games and played in them both.
In one I turned out for a Schoolteachers XI against an All Star XI and, once again, it was taken too seriously at times.
An example of this came when I placed a shot past the opposing goalkeeper Geoff Capes, the world's strongest man, but Ray Harford handled the ball on the line to prevent it going into the

Geoff Capes hates to be beaten
- is foul play imminent?

“I’ll see you after the match”
Geoff Capes fails to appreciate Tony winning a penalty

net for what would have been the opening goal. I was so incensed I ignored the fact that a big crowd was watching and strode up to hammer the penalty into the net, past the huge figure of Geoff Capes.

The Schoolteachers grimly hung on to the lead I had given them, not allowing Steve Coppell, Ossie Ardiles and Co. enough time and space to show off their skills. So I suggested to the referee that he give the All Stars a soft penalty, and once they had scored from the spot, their confidence came flooding back.

Suddenly Coppell and Ardiles were producing flashes of their old magic and they ran out easy winners.

But the Schoolteachers moaned like hell in the dressing room afterwards about the penalty decision!

I actually got to score a 'hat-trick' at Wembley without playing a game there! How is that possible, you may well ask.

Well, I was editor of Football Monthly, Britain's oldest soccer magazine, at the time and had been invited to write a special feature on the Veterans Cup Final at the old Wembley Stadium. Both teams were willing to name me as one of their substitutes, but were not so keen on the idea of actually bringing me on to play, having never seen me before. This, of course, was quite understandable.

I chose to be a substitute for the team which included former Nottingham Forest star Garry Birtles at centre-forward, and persuaded him to agree to come off two minutes from the end so that I could go on just to have the experience of playing at Wembley. But as the scores were still level in the 88th minute, his manager wouldn't let Garry do the switch.

Ironically, the other team suffered several injuries during the match and I would have got to play had I been a substitute for them!

So how did I score a hat-trick? That came when I converted three penalties out of three in the pre-match kick-about, and I was rather proud of myself because it was against a very good goalkeeper who was taking even the warm-up penalties very seriously.

Back in the Football Monthly office we scratched our heads to think of an appropriate headline for an event that, if I recall, did not produce a single goal in 90 minutes.

I am embarrassed to confess that we highlighted my experience in the story and came up with the heading: 'My Wembley penalty hat-trick.'

CHAPTER NINETEEN

# REDKNAPP'S LIE SHOWS HOW TOUGH OUR JOB CAN BE

Journalists get a lot of flack, some of which is fully deserved, but they have a very tough job in keeping the public informed, especially when they are lied to by the people they are interviewing. This was highlighted in Spurs manager Harry Redknapp's tax evasion trial in February.

Redknapp gave an interview to News of the World reporter Rob Beasley in February, 2009 in which he said that payments made by his then Portsmouth chairman Milan Mandaric to an account in Monaco were a bonus for the profit made on the sale of striker Peter Crouch.

But Redknapp told the court that he had lied to Beasley to prevent a story appearing in the Sunday tabloid as Spurs prepared to face Manchester United in the 2009 League Cup final.

Redknapp was jointly accused with Mandaric of colluding to conceal payments totalling £187,000 in a Monaco bank account named 'Rosie 47' after Harry's late dog.

The Crown claimed that the payments, made between 2002 and 2004, were taxable since they were employment-related.

Redknapp and Mandaric denied the charges, saying the money was an investment that had nothing to do with Redknapp's employment. Both men were found not guilty after waiting five agonising hours for the jury to give their verdict in a cliff hanging trial at Southwark Crown Court.

For once an emotionally drained Redknapp could not come up with a joke for his adoring media and public.

He has treated us to plenty in the past, the best of which have been:

"Even when they had Moore, Hurst and Peters, West Ham's average finish was about 17$^{th}$ position. It just shows how crap the other eight of us were"

"Hartson's got more previous than Jack the Ripper"

"Samassi Abou don't speak the English too good"

"By the look of him, he [Ian Dowie] must have headed a lot of balls"

"Where are we in relation to Europe? Not far from Dover"

"I sorted out the team formation last night lying in bed with the wife. When your husband's as ugly as me, you'd only want to talk football in bed."

On a serious note, Redknapp claimed that appearing with him in court would have killed his wife Sandra.

He said: "Going to jail did cross my mind. Nothing could compare with the court case. Once you've been through that there's nothing worse.

"The case made my wife Sandra ill - slaughtered her. It knocked her for six. She's soft. I wouldn't let her come to court - it would have killed her."

His ordeal reminded me of another court case involving a top football manager, former Manchester United boss Tommy Docherty, who brought a highly-publicised libel case in 1978 over remarks by Scottish international Willie Morgan to the effect that Docherty was, in his opinion, "about the worst manager there has ever been."

Docherty actually had a good record at Manchester United, but he dropped the case on the third day after claims that he had lied in evidence.

At the time I was Sports Editor of the Lancashire Evening Telegraph in Blackburn and attended a local dinner at which Docherty had been booked to speak immediately after the trial. There was deadly silence as he got up to talk, but he won the audience over and immediately had them in fits of laughter by saying: "You're not going to believe a word of this."

When Tommy and I chatted recently he came out with an updated quip about his court appearance by telling me: "I admitted to the judge I'd lied on oath, but he didn't believe me, either." And he added: "The guy operating the lift at the Old Bailey asked me if I was going down and I said 'I hope not'." No wonder I love talking to The Doc!

One of my favourite Docherty quotes came after he was sacked by Aston Villa chairman Doug Ellis. Tommy later recalled how his chairman had initially said he was right behind his manager. His response was: "I told him I'd sooner have him in front of me where I could see him."

And following his unsuccessful spell as manager of Rotherham United, Docherty declared: "I promised the chairman I'd get them out of the Second Division (now the Championship) and I did. I took them into the Third."

Other great Docherty jokes were:

"Elton John decided he wanted to rename Watford and call it Queen of the South."

"They offered me a handshake of £10,000 to settle amicably. I told them that they would have to be a lot more amicable than that."

Referring to Ray Wilkins: "He can't run, he can't tackle and he can't head the ball. The only time he goes forward is for the toss."

And on Paul Gascoigne: "He's a disgrace... 30 going on six!"

Having such a great sense of humour, and being prepared to poke fun at himself got The Doc out of some awkward situations during his long career as it has Redknapp, who I also found to be very entertaining at his post-match Press conferences - win, lose or draw!

Docherty is best remembered for his time at Manchester United, saving them from relegation and winning the Second Division when they were relegated the year after. There followed successive FA Cup final appearances, the latter a great 2-1 win over Liverpool to deny them the treble in 1976, but he was sacked a year later in July, 1977.

This was due mainly to pressure from players' wives after Docherty had an affair with the wife of club physio Laurie Brown. The fact that this was not some wild fling, and that Tommy had left his wife of 27 years to live with Mary Brown was not enough to save him.

He and Mary, 18 years his junior, showed their devotion to each other by marrying, and have enjoyed a very happy life together ever since.

At the age of 83, Tommy is still razor sharp and talks a lot of sense. The former Scotland manager knows what goes on in international football, and supports my view that former England boss Fabio Capello was stabbed in the back when he departed in February on the same day Redknapp was found not guilty in his court case.

Docherty told me: "Any manager would expect to be consulted prior to his employer sacking his captain.

"By not telling Capello of their intention to take the captaincy away from John Terry until after making their decision, the FA put their manager in an almost impossible situation.

"I find it hard to believe that they did not know Capello would feel forced to quit. I feel Capello was right to support Terry on the basis that a man is innocent until proved guilty. I wonder if the FA had a hidden agenda in not backing a manager who was costing them £6 million a year."

Docherty added: "Normally the FA would have been severely criticised for making yet another insensitive blunder and acting like a bunch of amateurs, but because many journalists and fans did not feel Capello was the right man for the job, the FA got away with it.

"The fact remains that Capello, despite making some mistakes, was a very capable manager who had the support of most of his players and he deserved a crack at the Euros after getting England to the finals. Sadly, I don't feel the current England players are good enough to win a major tournament."

During my career as a journalist, Docherty - and Redknapp - were always very friendly and co-operative with me. I remember when I took over as Head of Sport at Sunday Sport that our newly-appointed big name writer Peter Batt left just before our launch and I had to write the stories for the first issue myself.

We needed an explosive article that was going to be a 'must read' for most sports fans, and The Doc came up trumps by giving me an outspoken exclusive on which managers were in line for the sack.

Former England manager Bobby Robson was also very helpful when I was Sports Editor of the Fleet Street News Agency. I found two of his successors, Terry Venables and Glenn Hoddle, to be less free with their time.

Robson kindly granted me one-to-one exclusive interviews after his Press conferences because he knew that, as I worked for a freelance agency, I could not market the same quotes he had given to the rest of the media.

My one regret is that when I took my impressionable young son James along with me to one of Robson's Press conferences I did not introduce James to him properly because I was so anxious to get some quotes first.

In fact, Bobby told me he didn't have much time that day so I had to be quick which meant James never did get introduced to him.

CHAPTER TWENTY

# VIOLATED BY NEWS OF THE WORLD

I was very sad to see the demise of the News of the World, especially as I worked there for more than a year as a part-time sports sub-editor, being one of several 'Saturday casuals' brought in to help cope with the busiest day of a Sunday paper's week.

But I have no sympathy for those found guilty of phone hacking - in my day reporters would find out facts by asking probing questions, even if it meant standing around for hours to catch a few minutes (sometimes only seconds) with the people they needed to speak to.

The News of the World's publishers News International had to admit their guilt and pay out huge sums to many people whose phones were hacked into, including £300,000 in damages, plus the same amount in legal costs, to singer Charlotte Church and her parents.

The scandal left a lot of the hacking victims feeling violated as has been pointed out by Abi Titmuss, who I have referred to meeting earlier in this book.

Abi admitted that her career as a pin-up model before becoming a serious actress was mainly due to the media. But she stressed that the

Press had no right to be so intrusive to the point where her life was no longer her own.
She said: "The Press created me, but they almost destroyed me emotionally and my family.
"I knew for a  long time they were hacking my phone, but nobody believed me. I changed my number lots of times, but that didn't stop it.
"I've had journalists who I've met since say 'We used to make up things all the time'. My self esteem had become so low and I had become so unhappy because of what was happening.
"I sued News International for hacking my phone  - they thought they were untouchable."
Discussing the situation with Andrew Neil on BBC's 'This Week' in February, she explained: "The reason there was a public outcry was that if it was just celebrities who had their phones hacked people would have shrugged and it would not have been such a huge deal.
"But ordinary people were involved - grieving parents who never sought fame."
Abi was referring to the disgraceful case in which the parents of a murdered British teenager were given false hope that she was still alive.
The Leveson investigation was ordered after revelations that a private detective working for the News of the World hacked the phone of 13-year-old Milly Dowler while she was missing.
Milly's mother, Sally Dowler, described the moment she got through to her daughter's

previously full voicemail.
"It clicked through onto her voicemail, so I heard her voice... And it was just like, 'she has picked up her voicemails - she is alive'."
That was the final nail in the coffin of the News of the World, although it has, of course, been replaced on Sundays by its former sister paper The Sun.
Will the tabloid Press now be more responsible? I sincerely hope so, but, as Abi said: "The trouble with tabloid culture is that it requires a constant supply of victims like errant MPs, misbehaving footballers and fallen rock stars - when ordinary people become involved then things are different."

CHAPTER TWENTY-ONE

# WHY WE 'RUBBISHED' OUR OWN STORIES

My life at Sunday Sport in the late 1980's was bizarre, as you might imagine.

When I saw the advertisement seeking the 'Head of Sport' for a new national tabloid newspaper, I thought it would be a serious publication. Only after I landed the job did I fully realise that Sunday Sport was going to be a down market version of the Sun, with news pages crammed full of pictures of topless models and sexy stories.

I vowed to keep the sport serious so I was delighted when we took on Bobby Moore, and gave him the title of Sports Editor, with me being Assistant Editor in charge of sport. It meant I was the boss of England's 1966 World Cup-winning captain!

I promptly recruited other sports stars as columnists, including tennis ace Jo Durie and athlete Fatima Whitbread. I also brought in a host of former footballers such as John Charles, Peter Osgood, Alan Hudson, Tommy Smith and Frank McLintock to write Saturday match reports, all on a very small budget!

Before settling on Jo Durie I had approached Virginia Wade at the Wimbledon Championships.

But she appeared to be rather disdainful about the whole idea, and it seemed obvious the fee on offer would be so derisory to her that she'd almost certainly scoff at it.

Only after she said she wasn't interested and I was walking away did she call back to me: "Anyway, how much are you offering?"

I saved face by replying "You'll never know now, Virginia."

I also had the task of escorting models Samantha Fox and Linda Lusardi and DJ Tony Blackburn into a party Sunday Sport threw at Stringfellows night club. It was a tough job!

As I mentioned briefly in a previous chapter, there was a massive queue outside Stringfellows and I had to walk along it to rescue any VIPs who were supposed to gain immediate entrance.

One of the VIPs I found in the queue was Tony Blackburn, but by now the nightclub was packed. I told him: "Come with me, Tony, but if you think this is a big crowd outside just you wait until you get in. It's heaving with people." A lot of those people were scantily clad girls.

When Sunday Sport was launched in 1986 the staff would be instructed by our own management to phone up various radio shows and 'rubbish' ourselves by telling them how dreadful the paper's stories were. This was reverse psychology aimed at arousing listeners' interest so much that they felt compelled to buy the paper!

Sunday Sport would run ridiculous stories such as 'Women pregnant 60 years gives birth to old age pensioner'.

The paper printed what it claimed was a picture of a B-17 World War Two bomber plane on the moon. The photograph, supposedly taken from thousands of miles away, wasn't even blurred.

Sure enough, Sunday Sport readers wrote in to complain - but not about it being a faked picture! They pointed out that it was NOT a B-17, but a B-29.

And while other papers were asking whether the Queen should abdicate, Sunday Sport readers already knew it was a pointless debate because her body had allegedly been taken over by aliens years earlier.

Some of our readers even accepted our ludicrous claims that a double-decker London bus had been found frozen in the Antarctic ice and that Hitler was a woman.

Although I came to loathe the way all this distracted from our serious sports reporting, I was, nevertheless, proud that I was part of a dedicated editorial team which helped to launch a new national paper and build up a circulation of almost half a million from scratch.

We printed Sunday Sport from the offices of the Northampton Evening Chronicle each Saturday, and when we did our dummy run I was in charge of the whole sports operation.

This meant working with a completely new staff and having to get the paper on the printing presses an hour after the Saturday afternoon football programme had finished, including working out the league tables.

Editor-in-chief Mike Gabbert had suggested that we get famous former soccer players to report on matches so it was necessary for our sub-editors to speak to these personalities at half-time and again at the end of the game.

As a safety measure, I ensured that the personalities were sitting in the Press box next to qualified soccer writers, who telephoned over factual reports before handing the phone to the former players to give their opinions.

My team of sub-editors, a collection of freelance 'casuals', found it to be a frantic operation.

The staff of the Northampton Chronicle were sitting at the far end of their editorial offices having a laugh at our expense. But they weren't laughing when we brought out the first ever edition on time with everything in place.

Sunday Sport's publishers were David Sullivan and brothers David and Ralph Gold, with advertising the responsibility of Sullivan's protégé Karren Brady. The four of them went on to take control at Birmingham City Football Club and later West Ham United.

Sunday Sport was still going strong when I

departed in late 1988, together with the rest of the full-time sports staff, in protest at the farcical stories appearing in the paper's news pages. The final straw came when the news section warned that Aliens would invade the Wimbledon Lawn Tennis championships.

When it didn't happen, Sunday Sport refused to apologise. Instead, they ran another exclusive, saying that the Aliens were allergic to rain and the wet weather had foiled their planned invasion!

But a few years later the Sport and it's new sister publication Daily Sport began to lose their appeal and circulation dwindled. Sunday Sport's publication was suspended from April 1, 2011 after Sport Media Group ceased trading and appointed administrators, with all 90 staff being made redundant.

Former owner David Sullivan stepped in to buy Sunday Sport, but not the Daily Sport. Publication resumed on May 8, 2011 under a new company, Sunday Sport (2011) Ltd, and the paper took on its own website. But a full time staff of just eight occupied their new Manchester office which was a similar number to when we started back in 1986.

Despite all the young topless girls associated with Sunday Sport, I had been happy to spend my free time with a respectable divorced mother of three boys called Linda.

You may recall I mentioned how she did not recognise Frank Bruno when I took her to the Sports Personality of the Year awards at Wembley.

At the same event Linda was photographed with Nick Faldo, who she did recognise, and John Sillett, the manager of Coventry City, the shock team of the year after beating Spurs to win the 1987 FA Cup in their first ever final after 104 years of trying.

Sillett was standing next to Linda grinning as a picture was about to be taken when suddenly his smile changed to a rather pained expression after she had spoken to him.

"What on earth did you say to him?" I asked her as we walked away. "Nothing," she replied. "I just said 'I've got no idea who on earth you are'."

Sillett obviously had an ego and felt that people should know who he was. Indeed, the now portly, balding Sillett recalled in the build up to this year's FA Cup third round: "I'm reminded of our cup win every time I walk down the street in Coventry, Liverpool and all sorts of places. I'm recognised all the time. People say 'Hey, Cup Final 1987'. They even remember the date."

The likeable former Sky Blues boss, who gave Coventry their only FA Cup final triumph, revealed that by beating Manchester United on route to Wembley they almost brought about the demise of United manager Alex Ferguson.

Sillett disclosed: “Alex said ‘It’s the nearest I’ve ever been to getting the sack’.”
John claimed that Coventry’s second equaliser in a 3-2 extra-time victory was “the best goal to be scored at Wembley - a diving header by Keith Houchen from a magnificent cross by Dave Bennett.”
Perhaps a slight exaggeration, John!

CHAPTER TWENTY-TWO

# 'I WAS DRAINED AND DEPRESSED' SAYS FLINTOFF

Sports stars today are treated like kings compared to those of bygone years. But, with the mega bucks, comes more media attention, stress and sometimes depression.

Among those who have suffered from the intense pressures have been cricket ace Freddie Flintoff and footballer-turned-actor Vinnie Jones.

I have met them both and saw some evidence of the stress that fan adoration and the media spotlight can place on them.

I was with Flintoff only briefly when my newspaper was invited to interview him at a book signing so I went along with my colleague Ross Basham, who was covering the event.

We were staggered to see such a massive crowd turn up to buy Flintoff's book and have it signed by the England hero himself. It took him ages to sign all the books, pose for pictures and answer questions.

Freddie was charming, but I thought I detected behind the smiles a trace of anxiety from the Ashes hero, who has recently revealed that the pressure of Test cricket left him fighting depression and led to booze binges.

Flintoff has admitted to being at his lowest ebb in 2007 when he was sacked as England's vice captain following a drunken Pedalo ride during the World Cup.

He confessed: "Sportsmen experience unbelievable highs and dramatic lows.

"You never think that the lows could turn into depression - but for some it all gets too much."

Talking about that Caribbean nightmare in a BBC1 documentary, 'The Hidden Side of Sport' screened on January 11, 2012, he said: "I didn't know what I was doing, and all I was thinking about on the field and throughout that World Cup was that I wanted to retire.

"When I took wickets I used to like a celebration. But on that trip I just stood there. I couldn't muster the energy to do anything."

It was all a far cry from when he became a national hero by inspiring England's Ashes triumph in 2005. But his fortunes changed dramatically when he captained England to a humiliating 5-0 defeat in the Ashes series of 2006-7 in Australia.

Flintoff revealed that on Christmas Eve 2006 he cried his eyes out and told his dad he couldn't take it any more - that he couldn't keep playing. He added: "I dusted myself down and carried on, but I was never the same player again."

He confessed that he turned to drink long before he quit playing in 2010 through injury.

Tony and colleague Ross Basham join Freddie at his book signing.

Freddie admitted: "I was so low at the time (of the Pedalo incident) it might have pushed me over the edge."

Vinnie Jones had previously told how he had been hit by suicidal depression after biting a journalist in 1998.

He said: "I'd let everybody down. I took a gun to the woods with the intention of firing it. I was tired of causing people stress - it was a cheap way out, but I did think everyone would be better off if I was out of the way and stopped causing them trouble."

His dog saved him from pulling the trigger. The Jack Russell terrier had followed him, and the dog's pleading look caused Jones to abandon his suicide mission.

Hard man Jones, a member of the Wimbledon Crazy Gang who helped the Dons win the 1998 FA Cup final against all the odds, was sent off 12 times in his career.

I interviewed Vinnie after one of his on-field misdemeanours caused him to see red once again, and I feared that my questions about the incident would cause him to erupt with fury. Fortunately, Jones had calmed down by the time we spoke and I saw the other, humorous side of him. We finished up having a good laugh!

CHAPTER TWENTY-THREE

# JIMMY WHITE AND THE WAISTCOAT

I spent almost four very happy years as Controller of Information at BSkyB and often joked about having 200 people working under me because I was on the third floor and they were on the two floors below me!

My main job was performing an important public relations exercise to increase awareness of the Eurosport channel. I did this by arranging a variety of events and issuing a stream of press releases, many of them containing interviews I carried out with sports stars who appeared on Eurosport programmes.

I was responsible for publicising one of Sky and Eurosport's biggest sports events, the first World Snooker Masters, which was the richest snooker tournament to be held, with £1 million prize money, and the first to feature women players as well as men at that level.

The initial Press Conference in November, 1990 saw me interview on camera world champions Stephen Hendry and Alison Fisher, Jimmy White, promoter Barry Hearn and presenter Dickie Davies.

In order to add a touch of glamour, it was decided to let the contestants wear brightly coloured, trendy waistcoats.

So I contacted a Savile Row tailor and arranged to hire about 25 waistcoats from him. Jimmy White, then one of the top players in the world, look a shine to one of them and was reluctant to part with it at the end of the tournament until I told him how much it would cost him!

Football manager Ron Atkinson was another who gave me a problem. He had agreed to pose in a Sky cap for a publicity picture at the next match his Sheffield Wednesday team played in London, but when the photographer and I approached him before kick-off at Charlton, he said there wasn't enough time and he would do it in Sheffield instead!

Atkinson wasn't made aware that, when news of this got back to the Sky office, concern was expressed about whether perhaps we might want someone more flexible to be part of our team!

One of my ideas at Sky was to promote our 1990 World Cup coverage by creating our own man-sized version of the competition mascot Ciao.

So I hired a tailor to make us a costume, complete with a football-shaped head, and then all I needed was someone to wear it. There were no volunteers which meant I had to don it myself to appear on TV as a giant mascot.

The person who actually found the tailor to carry out this task was my mother! I needed a temporary assistant who I knew I could rely on so took on my mum as a 'casual' shortly after she had retired from her job as a secretary.

I didn't tell anybody in the Sky office that my new assistant was my mother, but they may have guessed when she kept straightening my tie and on one occasion told me to adjust my trousers!

My job sometimes enabled me to help promote worthy causes, and I organised a charity football match in which we filmed the likes of Ossie Ardiles and Steve Coppell. Afterwards I interviewed both Ossie and Steve on camera.

Surprisingly, I did not have much contact with the long-serving anchormen of Sky's football

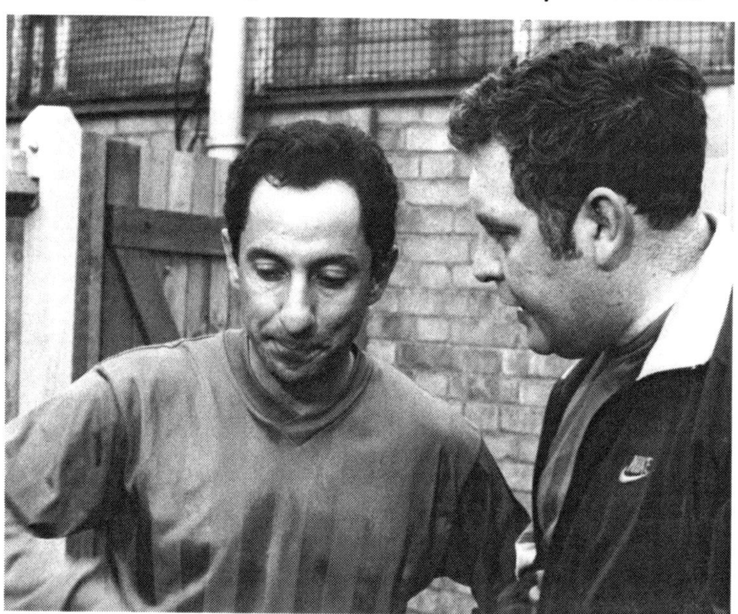

"Do you still miss playing for 'Tottingham', Ossie?"

coverage, Richard Keys and Andy Gray, who were hauled off air in January, 2011 as punishment for sexist comments about a female football official.

Keys resigned after Gray lost his job over sexist remarks made off air but caught on tape.

The pair were originally disciplined for making sexist remarks about the female assistant referee Sian Massey before a match between Wolves and Liverpool. They were off air but recorded on tape and it was leaked to the media.

Gray was dismissed after new footage came to light that showed him making suggestive remarks to a female co-host. The pressure to take action against Keys, too, increased when another clip appeared to show him talking in sexiest terms about a former girlfriend of the pundit Jamie Redknapp. Keys resigned soon afterwards.

It's amazing to reflect how swiftly the axe can fall on even those playing massive roles in a multi-million pound industry.

As most of my time was devoted to public relations at Eurosport, I appeared on Sky sports channels only a few times, and ironically most of my television appearances came on BBC News 24 some years later. The Beeb engaged me as an early morning analyst, commenting on the sports news of the week and handing out criticism where necessary as I did to Manchester

United boss Alex Ferguson over his famous boot kicking rage which injured his own player David Beckham.

One of my TV appearances on an evening programme nearly didn't happen because of the fussiness of the producer. I was due to talk about the England football team and at the 11th hour this producer got the bright idea that I should be standing in front of the twin towers of Wembley Stadium.

So he sent a car and off we sped from South East London, in rush hour traffic, with only an hour to get there for my scheduled slot.

It was a mad rush and we only made it with a few minutes of the programme remaining. It still amazes me that the producer risked missing out on the whole thing just for the sake of having Wembley in the background!

I also used to be on screen regularly as a guest on Mirror Group Newspapers' fledgling LIVE TV British cable television channel, set up in 1995.

The channel's boss was Kelvin MacKenzie, who after editing the Sun moved to BSkyB but left them within a few months.

The station had previously been headed by Janet Street-Porter, who wanted to establish LIVE TV as an alternative, youth-orientated channel. She clashed with MacKenzie over programme content and soon departed, leaving him in sole charge.

MacKenzie went downmarket by introducing nightly editions of 'Topless Darts', featuring bare-chested women playing darts on a beach, 'The Weather in Norwegian' (with a young, blonde, bikini-clad Scandinavian woman presenting weather forecasts in both English and Norwegian), and stock exchange reports from Tiffany, a young female presenter who would strip as she read out the latest share prices.

I appeared on the channel's more conservative programmes, commenting on various sports topics before ending up playing some daft game in a one-to-one challenge against the celebrity guest I was appearing with. This hardly brought me countrywide fame because the station had a budget of only £2,000 an hour and was never watched by more than an average of 200,000 viewers.

CHAPTER TWENTY-FOUR

# 'WHY I MARRIED JACKLIN DESPITE HIS FLING'

Sport can play hell with married life - and golfers on tour are some of the biggest 'victims'.

I spent a long conversation sympathising with Scottish star Sandy Lyle about his marriage ending in divorce, and, after speaking to former Open Champion Tony Jacklin and his second wife, I could even understand him having an affair with a teenage girl soon after the death of his first wife.

But I had less sympathy for fellow Brit Nick Faldo over his marriage break-ups and none at all for American icon Tiger Woods, whose wife suddenly discovered that the world's most successful golfer loved playing around so much he sometimes had as many birdies off the course as on it!

I was given an exclusive interview by Jacklin and his second wife Astrid, which made a double-page spread, containing my by-line, in the Daily Star in September 1989.

Astrid, who married Britain's most successful Ryder Cup captain only eight months after his first wife Vivien died of a brain haemorrhage while driving her car in Spain, told me how they coped when death struck again by depriving them of a baby son.

Norwegian-born Astrid, formerly married to Bee Gees guitarist Alan Kendall, also spoke about what it was like to live with the ghost of Tony's first marriage.

She said: "Vivien is always going to be part of our lives. I realise that when you have loved someone for so long, you don't forget them just because they are no longer alive.

"If you've spent more than 20 years with them and had three kids with them, they're still part of you and the memories will always be there."

Astrid had to come through other traumas soon after Tony breezed into her life. She recalled: "Within two weeks of me meeting Tony in Spain, the story of his fling with a teenage waitress broke.

"He'd already told me about it, and I accepted it as something that happened when he was still beside himself with grief over his wife's death."

Despite the 'sex romp' headlines following 16-year-old waitress Donna Nethven's kiss-and-tell revelations about the three-month affair which started six weeks after Vivien's death, Astrid insisted: "I had complete belief in Tony."

Jacklin said: "I have been tremendously fortunate to find someone so understanding. If Astrid hadn't been so right I wouldn't have asked her not to go back to America after knowing her only three days."

He and Astrid also had to overcome the tragedy of losing their baby in July, 1989.

When Astrid began having contractions four months early during the British Open in Troon they needed to get to London quickly to see her doctor, so Jack Nicklaus lent them his private jet. But nothing could be done and Astrid miscarried.

Tony tried to be philosophical. He said: "I suppose life is kind of like golf - It's a little like Trevino's chip-in. Anything can happen to you, any time, so what's the point of trying to understand it? You can't make sense of it anyway, so why try?"

When I met Faldo, the winner of six majors, we did not touch on the subject of his marriage break-ups, but I spoke in depth to Lyle about his divorce.

Sandy, who triumphed in the British Open in 1985 and the Masters in 1988, was deeply upset by his split from his wife Christine, also a professional golfer, in 1987.

He told me: "Golf has made me a lot of money, yet it has cost me a divorce and so much upset. But I'm lucky to have my kids."

I tried to console him with words of sympathy and encouragement about how better things lay in store for him. I also threw in a joke: "Man is not complete until he's married and then he's finished. But practice makes perfect."

Faldo tried to laugh off his marriage problems with a few jokes of his own.

His best were: "We were happily married for eight months - unfortunately we were married for four and a half years!" and "I never advise anyone to go to war or to get married."

Faldo met his first wife, Melanie Rockall, when he was 21. They wed in 1979, but five years later they split up when she discovered he was having a relationship with his manager's secretary, Gill Bennett.

He then married Bennett in 1986, and the couple had three children, Natalie, Matthew, and Georgia. They parted in 1995 after Faldo became involved with 20-year-old American golfing student Brenna Cepelak.

The three-year affair with Cepelak ended when Faldo met Valerie Bercher. The spurned Cepelak showed her anger by pounding Faldo's Porsche 959 with a golf club, causing £10,000 damage.

Faldo's relationship with Bercher, a Swiss PR agent, began in 1998 when they met at the European Masters golf tournament. She left her fiancé Olivier Delaloye, married Faldo in July, 2001 at his Windsor home, and two years later they had a daughter, Emma Scarlet.

But it was announced in May, 2006 that Faldo had filed for divorce and again the Press were having a field day at his expense.

Little wonder that journalists are not his favourite

people. But when I helped to entertain him at a Sports Writers Association dinner, where I was a member of the organising committee, he was at his most affable and charming.

I feel that Faldo got off lightly compared to Tiger Woods over the repercussions of his relationships with women, especially regarding the damage to his pocket.

Woods paid a very heavy price for cheating several times on wife Elin Nordegren, who divorced him in August, 2010.

The Swedish former model is believed to have been paid £100 million as part of the settlement and Tiger's reputation was severely tarnished. But he had nobody to blame but himself!

CHAPTER TWENTY-FIVE

# CURTAIN WENT UP AS SINGER WAS BEING SPANKED

Some of the biggest names in show business have suffered from stage fright, including Barbra Streisand, Rod Stewart, Colin Firth, Geoffrey Rush, Frankie Howerd and even the late Sir Laurence Olivier.

Stephen Fry revealed that it forced him to contemplate suicide, while singer Carly Simon tried to overcome the problem by having her bottom spanked!

TV presenter, award winning actor and singer Matthew Kelly has also been plagued by stage fright, as he told me when we chatted at Richmond Theatre with Rula Lenska.

He said: “It is something which many actors and singers suffer from. I still get scared about performing as an actor, and many years ago I lost my nerve for singing on stage.”

Kelly, best known as the host of ITV’s ‘Stars In Their Eyes’, expanded on the subject when appearing on the ‘Alan Titchmarsh Show’ on ITV in March. He explained: “If you are nervous and get actual stage fright your singing voice is the first thing to go.

“It’s awful. Even now I’m terrified of going on stage when I’m doing a play. Every morning I

A confident looking Matthew Kelly has suffered from stage fright which he appears to have passed on to Tony

wake up and think 'Please God, don't make me do that.' But the minute you set foot on stage it's the greatest ride of your life.

"Actors are the most wonderful people to be with – they're funny, they're kind, they're supportive, they're generous – and they're bonkers!"

But Barbra Streisand, whose stage fright caused her to stay away from the concert stage for more than 25 years, didn't appear to show much support to the late Dudley Moore when, in 1995, she fired him from the film she was directing, 'The Mirror Has Two Faces', for having trouble remembering his lines.

It was devastating for Dudley, who two years later had open-heart surgery. He suffered four strokes, and doctors discovered a build up of calcium on his brain, an irreversible condition worsened by drugs and alcohol. He died in 2002 aged 66.

Miss Streisand, who probably did not know about his health problems when she worked with Moore, has always been a notorious perfectionist. She had said years earlier while emerging as a new teenage sensation: "I wasn't trying to be difficult - it just came naturally."

Her sometimes seemingly harsh reactions pale into insignificance when compared to the bitchy Joan Rivers, who made some terrible remarks about a fellow contestant, poker player Annie Duke, on the American version of 'The Apprentice' this year. But I would have thought Miss Streisand might have been more understanding with Dudley Moore, especially as she had also failed to remember her lines on one memorable occasion.

She had forgotten the lyrics to one of her songs during a 1967 Central Park concert, which resulted in her no longer performing live for almost three decades.

She said: "Some performers forget the words all the time, but they somehow have humour about it. I didn't have a sense of humour about it. I was quite shocked."

Even Sir Laurence Olivier, the greatest actor of his time, worried frantically that he would fail to remember his lines as he reached late middle age. It got so bad that the stage manager had to push him on stage every night in one run at London's National Theatre.

Stephen Fry actually walked out on the West End play 'Cell Mates' in 1995 and contemplated suicide.

The comedian and writer revealed: "I went into my garage, sealed the door with a duvet and got into my car. I sat there for at least two hours, with my hands on the ignition key. It was a suicide attempt – not a cry for help."

But instead of gassing himself, Fry fled to Belgium. He recalled: "I really believed I would never come back to England. But after a week I secretly returned and went to hospital where a doctor told me that I'm bipolar."

Fry, speaking in a BBC2 documentary about being a depressive, added: "For the first time, at the age of 37, I had a diagnosis that explained the massive highs and miserable lows I've lived with all my life."

His walk-out after only three days in the part of KGB agent George Blake meant that Simon Gray's play, which also starred Rik Mayall, was killed off.

Speaking of his decision to go AWOL, Fry said: "That was play fright, not stage fright - it's a very different thing."

One actor, Ian Holm, actually gave up during a performance! He walked off stage and refused to return in 'The Iceman Cometh' in 1976. He explained in a 1998 interview: "Something just snapped. Once the concentration goes, the brain literally closes down."

Colin Firth and Geoffrey Rush have also admitted to suffering stage fright, which is doubly ironic after the acclaim they both received in 'The King's Speech', the Oscar-winning film about the chronic stammer of George VI (Firth) and his treatment with an Australian speech therapist (Rush).

Firth recalled how on opening night of his last stage appearance at the Donmar Warehouse in 1999 he became so scared that he locked himself in the toilet. Then he went out of the theatre to get some air, and accidentally shut the fire door behind him, five minutes before he was due on stage.

He recalled: "I was forced to go round the front of the theatre, through the audience – the very people I was terrified of facing." In his panic he couldn't remember the pass code to get backstage and had to plead to be allowed in.

Rush admitted having similar problems in the early 1990's. He recalled: "I suffered dread-inducing panic attacks before going on stage - then I got an international film career and they sort of disappeared."

Rod Stewart was so nervous when performing at New York's Fillmore East Theatre back in 1968 that he sang the whole of the first song from behind a pile of speakers.

The most bizarre method I've heard about for over-coming stage freight is that used by singer Carly Simon. She resorted to poking herself in the hand with safety pins, and having her bottom spanked before performing live.

But her secret ritual was accidentally revealed in the most embarrassing manner when she appeared at a concert in 1996 to mark then U.S. President Bill Clinton's 50th birthday.

Simon, already a popular recording artist, with a number of hit songs including 'Anticipation', 'You're So Vain' and 'Nobody Does It Better', confessed: "The orchestra's horn section all took turns spanking me. But during the spank the curtain went up."

The tall, attractive singer-songwriter, with the most sexy of pouts, whose admirers are said to include Jeremy Irons, Mick Jagger, Jack Nicholson, Kris Kristofferson and Cat Stevens, must have looked quite a sight. I wonder what Bill Clinton said to her afterwards!

CHAPTER TWENTY-SIX

# STAR-STRUCK ELVIS WAS AN EMBARRASSMENT

One of my contacts in show business told me that Elvis Presley was so much in awe of Tom Jones that he was like a star-struck fan.

Elvis also became an embarrassment to friends years later during the last 18 months of his life, when he was bloated, confused and liable to mood swings due to his dependency on prescription drugs.

It is claimed that the King of Rock 'n Roll went from being the iconic figure everybody wanted to be with to a person some friends would cross the street to avoid. He then became reclusive and chose to be on his own.

I was first given an insight into the sad situation during one of my trips to Las Vegas. I was told that there had been signs in Presley's concert performances of his decline. He mumbled introductions, sang the wrong lyrics and looked uncoordinated in his movements on stage.

My contact, who has big show business connections but preferred to be unnamed, told me how embarrassing this was for his friends. He said: "Some stayed loyal and some did not, while Elvis pushed other friends away. He was sad that Tom Jones, who he idolised, was no longer in the States. Presley had seemed to be in awe of Jones - just like a star-struck fan, to the point it became excessive."

It is believed that Sir Tom and Elvis did not see each other for the last 18 months of Presley's life. Jones said: "I didn't realise how ill he was. The first thing that hit me after he died was that I should have gone to see him."

Presley and Jones had met in 1965 at the Paramount film stage, when Elvis was filming 'Paradise, Hawaiian Style' and became very close, especially while Tom was starring in Vegas. Night after night, Elvis would turn up to watch Tom perform and often join him on stage. Sometimes Jones did not seem to appreciate it and told his road manager: "Hide the spare microphone - Presley is in."

A further indication that Elvis was fixated came when he sang to the Welshman while Tom was in the shower naked by leaning over the cubicle door in the star's changing room!

Following Presley's death on August 16, 1977 at the age of 42, primarily from a heart attack, Jones paid a warm tribute to him. The Welsh heartthrob said: "We were friends until just before he died. We had worked Vegas a lot together. He came to see me at The Flamingo in '68, because he said he wanted to make a comeback, live in Vegas, after not singing live for years.

"He felt that I was the closest thing to him - I had a similar approach. My stage presence, he felt, was very similar to his. So he said to me, 'You were very successful in Vegas, I want to watch you - I want to see what you do'. It gave him more confidence to make a comeback.

"I think he was the only person I've spoken to who felt the same way about music as myself, as far as versatility is concerned. He loved ballads as well as rock 'n' roll - he loved Gospel, he loved pop. We would sit in the suite and talk about music... and we would sing, mostly jam."

Before his decline, Presley was the greatest singer in the world, and his good looks were the envy of everyone in show business.

It was tragic that towards the end of his life he became obese and was so constipated that he would go days without visiting the bathroom. Unfortunately, many now remember him in his bloated state.

In contrast, Marilyn Monroe, who was just 36 when she was found dead on August 5, 1962, was still glamorous and is thought of as having been the most desirable woman in the world.

Marilyn died of an overdose from Barbiturates, but it is still a mystery as to whether she took her own life, either intentionally or by accident, or she was murdered.

Marilyn is renowned for her renditions of the songs 'Happy Birthday' and 'I Wanna Be Loved

By You'- and she sang the latter to me while sitting seductively on my lap! Unfortunately, the Marilyn I refer to was a gorgeous look-alike doing a tribute act in Bexhill-on-Sea!

I never got to meet Diana Dors, whose picture I plastered on my bedroom wall as a teenager, but getting to talk to the world's greatest boxer of all time, Muhammad Ali, and play football with the legendary George Best and Bobby Moore was pretty damn good.

Another highlight was getting to perform with one of my favourite comedians, Jimmy Carr, who called me up on stage to take part in a sketch as part of his show in the Edinburgh Festival.

I was required to collapse dramatically and, upon doing so, was berated by Jimmy for my pathetic acting attempt. But, thinking that attack was the best form of defence, I decided to engage in a verbal battle with the man who is famous for his offensive 'put downs'.

I got carried away and told him that the water bottle he was drinking from was the nearest he was going to get to a Perrier, the award that comedians craved at the Edinburgh Festival. Exchanging insults with the quick-witted Carr was taking a big risk, but he liked my joke and let me off lightly.

CHAPTER TWENTY-SEVEN

# ROWLING AND LLOYD WEBBER WERE SUED

My adventure fantasy book 'The Secret Potion' has been hailed by author Jessica Duchen and actress June Whitfield as an ideal follow up to Harry Potter – but I did not lift any of author J.K. Rowling's story lines or ideas.

Ironically, it is Rowling, probably the most successful and wealthiest author in the world, who has had to defend herself against charges of plagiarism.

A law suit was brought in 2002 by American author Nancy Stouffer, who claimed that there was a striking resemblance between her character 'Larry Potter' and Rowling's 'Harry Potter'. Although it was accepted that there were similarities between the spectacle-wearing Larry Potter and Harry Potter, Stouffer, whose books were published in the 1980's, lost her case and an appeal three years later.

More recently the estate of Adrian Jacobs, a writer who died in 1997, brought a plagiarism case against Rowling, but it was dismissed by a U.S. Judge after the estate's lawyers failed to meet a deadline to pay the first portion of a $2.6 million security fund mandated by a British court if the case should go to trial.

The claim was that Rowling repeated parts of Jacobs's 'Willie the Wizard' in 'Harry Potter and the Goblet of Fire'.The lawyers acting on behalf of his estate referred to the fact that Jacob's book involved a school for wizards and wizards travelling on trains. Rowling said she had never heard of Willie the Wizard before the copyright claim was taken out.

There have also been many copyright infringement cases brought by musicians and composers. Andrew Lloyd Webber was sued in 1998 by Baltimore songwriter Ray Repp, who claimed that the theme song from 'The Phantom of The Opera' was taken from his song 'Till You'. But a jury cleared Webber of plagiarism.

There were also claims that Phantom closely resembled some of the musical phrases in Puccini's opera 'The Girl of the Golden West' and the Puccini estate sued Webber. The suit was settled out of court, with the details not being made public.

It is hard to prove plagiarism because it can be claimed that most pieces of work bare some resemblance to something else on the basis that most things have already been thought of before. But there is, of course, a huge difference between a writer being influenced by another author or composer – and lifting someone else's work almost completely.

Actor and TV presenter Matthew Kelly, who I

once chatted to at a theatre function, which I referred to earlier, recently gave an insight into how he is influenced by other performers.

Speaking on 'The Alan Titchmarsh Show' on ITV, he said: "People always say never watch other actors do the part you are going to play. But I always watch them. I nick all the good bits.

"When I was doing 'Who's Afraid of Virginia Woof' people said 'don't watch Richard Burton do it'. Now, am I ever going to do it like Richard Burton? I'd be more like Elizabeth Taylor.

"It helps you to learn to watch others. There was a great line in a play about Eric Morecambe – 'There's nothing original until you make it your own'. I think that's absolutely true so that's how I justify my 'plagiarism'."

CHAPTER TWENTY-EIGHT

# CLAIRE SWEENEY WAS CHATTED UP BY U.S. PRESIDENT

Few women would deliberately put on two stones in six weeks, but actress and singer Claire Sweeney did!

The then 37-year-old Liverpudlian piled on the pounds in 2009 for a TV documentary called 'My Big Fat Diet' as she soared from 9st 12lb to 11st 10lb.

She told me: "I would eat pizzas, chicken, chips and Eggs Benedict. I got so fat, some people thought I was pregnant."

But being larger had it's advantages because men found her more ample breasts a big attraction, and those guys who had previously thought the gorgeous star was out of their league suddenly felt confident enough to approach her.

Claire said: "My bra size went from a 'C' cup to a 'G' cup. My boobs were magnificent and I'd never been chatted up by so many men."

One of those who tried out a chat-up line on her when she was in her trimmer shape was Bill Clinton while he was U.S. President, but Claire wasn't impressed.

She was wearing a cheeky Dangerous Liaisons-style costume at a fancy dress party in Russia, hosted by Cliff Richard, when Clinton approached her, dressed as an admiral.

Sweeney, who was at the party with her boyfriend Tony Hibbard, told Channel Five's 'The Wright Stuff': "Clinton came over and started chatting me up. I thought: 'You dirty dog'."

Despite being told by his bodyguard that it was time to go, the 62-year-old President refused to do so and returned to talk to her.

The conversation went as follows:

Claire: 'You don't want to go, do you?'

Clinton:'How can you tell?'

Claire:'Because your left leg is dancing'."

Clinton allegedly told her: 'My middle leg will be dancing soon!'

Sweeney joked: "I shook his hand, but decided I was going home with a clean dress that night!"

White House intern Monica Lewinsky had claimed that her blue dress had been soiled by The President during their affair in 1997.

CHAPTER TWENTY-NINE

# MILLION-TO-ONE SHOT NOT REPEATED AT ROULETTE TABLE

Getting a free honeymoon trip to Las Vegas, New Orleans and Hawaii sounds incredible – and so it was! But things didn't work out so well when I tried to uphold my part of the bargain with travel company Kuoni.

When my wife-to-be Heather and I were planning our wedding in 2000 I hit on the idea of arranging our honeymoon as a Press facility trip.

It came about because when I was making one of my regular appearances on BBC News 24 as a sports pundit I noticed the name Jeremy Skidmore on their schedule.

Jeremy had worked with me on the notorious Sunday Sport years earlier and was now editor of a travel magazine, so I felt he should be in a position to commission an article from me.

Tracking him down took longer than I expected, but then I had an amazing stroke of good fortune. I was covering a soccer match between Charlton Athletic and Wolves one Saturday afternoon for The People and rushed into a newsagent's shop near The Valley shortly before kick-off to buy a paper.

There in the shop was the very contact I needed. No, not the travel magazine, nor one of their representatives, but Jeremy Skidmore himself! The chances of that happening were a million to one – even allowing for the fact that Jeremy was going to the same match as a devoted Wolves fan.

It convinced me that this was meant to be – and perhaps was a sign that I would enjoy the same sort of luck at the gambling tables in Vegas.

Jeremy agreed to me writing a feature for him on the basis that it would have a new slant as Heather were older honeymooners in our 50s.

I did an excellent deal with Kuoni that, in exchange for the coverage I would be providing, they would give me a free tailor-made holiday to the three dream locations of Vegas, New Orleans and Hawaii – and Heather a reasonable discount.

Heather and I had a fabulous time, including upgrades to a wonderful suite in a luxury hotel in New Orleans, and so I was able to write a very positive review – too positive as it turned out.

Jeremy explained that I had been too gushing in my praise, and, as the editor of a travel magazine that was read by the trade, he needed to paint a more balanced picture.

So I re-wrote the article, which was still very complimentary, but now also focused on those holiday features that could have been slightly improved upon.

Jeremy liked the story and asked me to be patient as he felt it would be diplomatic to let his Features Editor decide when to use it. Unfortunately, within weeks, Jeremy had left the travel magazine, and the Features Editor chose not to use an article which she had been presented with by her former editor, rather than commissioning herself.

I was left with the unenviable task of explaining the situation to the Press Officer of Kuoni and leaving them to negotiate with the new editor to use the article.

Despite the concessions given to us, including complimentary tickets to top shows, our stay in Las Vegas still cost me a lot of money - in gambling.

When we arrived at the Mirage Hotel, Heather was tired and wanted to have a sleep so I went down to the casino alone to play roulette. Needless to say, I did not enjoy the same good fortune that had brought me into contact with my old mate 'Skidders' back in Charlton.

I tried out my 'system' based on the belief that it was most unlikely the roulette ball would land on the same colour ten times in succession. So, after waiting for four blacks to come up in a row, I started betting on red and tripled my stake every time I lost.

The problem was that the Mirage casino imposed

a higher minimum stake on even-money bets than casinos in England - so continually trebling up became expensive.

I soon ran out of dollars and the croupier held up the game while I went across to a booth to get around £300 exchanged in order that I could again triple my bet on the next spin of the wheel. It made no difference and I kept losing – probably £500 in all. Some system, eh?

When I sheepishly returned to our bedroom Heather asked me why I looked rather depressed. I didn't have the heart to tell her the full story. And just blurted out that I'd had some bad luck in the casino during the half an hour I had been away!

Heather eventually dug the truth out of me and said: "Never mind, darling. Now I won't feel guilty when I spend lots at the shops!"

Pre-planning is always important, and everything, including the connecting flights, went like clockwork. But Heather was not too impressed with my decision to arrange for an inhabitant of Las Vegas – a friend of a friend in London – to show us around.

Our 'guide' Robert, a larger-than-life Texan, complete with cowboy hat and boots, proved to be an extremely helpful gay guy, who seemed to take rather a shine to me. He insisted I sit at the front of his Cadillac with him on our sight-seeing trips and that I go to a hotel to take part in an organised card game with him while Heather was 'packed off'' to the shops. Needless to say, he gave me far more of his attention than he did my lovely bride!

Incidentally, the card session resulted in more losses and taught me that gambling is usually a mug's game.

Ironically, Heather was also 'overlooked' when we went to China and climbed the Great Wall. It was a sweltering hot day and our Chinese tour guide, aware that a big fellow like me was struggling with the steep slope as we approached the Wall, decided to give me a hand. So he got behind me and pushed me up the cobbled hill. What he didn't notice – and neither did I - was that Heather, who had been suffering with a virus, was lagging behind and close to fainting!

Our superb holiday to three cities in China (and Hong Kong) was also with Kuoni and I was pleased to be able to write a very positive review about it.

The only other time I had difficulty in delivering what I had promised to a travel company for a Press facility trip was when I was at Sunday Sport.

I had persuaded the Press Officer at Thomas Cook to give me a free holiday to Hong Kong, Singapore and Bangkok in exchange for a prominent feature story, and this was with the blessing of our unconventional Editor-in-chief

Mike Gabbert.

But upon my return, the sometimes eccentric Gabbert told me on Press day that he had a space to fill on a news page and wanted to shove my holiday article in it. When I saw that the space was only two columns wide, in the middle of the page, with no room for a picture, I was horrified.

I told Gabbert that we could not throw a holiday feature story away like this when we had a commitment to the travel company. But Mike, whose stubborn streak had seen him play a key part in The People uncovering the soccer match fixing scandal involving England players Peter Swan and Tony Kay, along with David Layne, in 1964, would not budge. He even used a frivolous headline about how I had bought a cheap suit in Bangkok.

I was horrified - and so was the Press Officer at Thomas Cook. But I retrieved the situation by arranging for a double-page feature to be used the following week, with Thomas Cook offering our readers a £50 discount on bookings for long haul holidays.

Although Gabbert was a great journalist, his insistence on sometimes trivialising stories and putting a sexual slant on them, as he did with a news item about an attractive female racing driver who was trying to take her sport seriously, caused a few ripples in our otherwise excellent relationship.

When he left Sunday Sport to become Editor of the Daily Star in 1987 he would have taken me with him, but the Star were based in Manchester and I had a commitment, as a divorced parent, to look after my son James, who lived with me near London.

It was just as well I did not go with Mike. Some of the existing Daily Star staff were opposed to their new editor from Sunday Sport, who had been foisted upon them, and this became immediately obvious when Gabbert gave his first editorial briefing.

Apparently, one of the senior female staffers told him in front of her colleagues that if he expected her to 'make up' readers' letters, as she reckoned he had done at Sunday Sport, then he would be greatly disappointed. Not to be outdone, Mike said in a loud stage whisper to one of his assistants "Find me someone who will."

I urged him not to take the Star too far down-market, but he insisted on packing it with girlie pictures and sex-orientated stories.

Advertising and circulation nose-dived and within months Gabbert had been sacked.

CHAPTER THIRTY

# HANKY-PANKY IN THE OFFICE WAS CUT SHORT

As a teenage reporter I once used the office for some 'hanky-panky' which back-fired on me badly and ended in embarrassment.

I had taken a young lady to the cinema one evening and afterwards we called in the office of my then paper the Kentish Times in Bromley to make a phone call.

One thing led to another and, after some passionate kisses, I cleared one of the editorial desks so that this delightful girl and I could get a little bit more physical. If I remember rightly, it was not long before an item of clothing was loosened.

But, obviously unbeknownst to me, John, our chief reporter at that time, couldn't sleep because he feared he had left the office fire on. So he told his wife he was getting out of bed and returning to his office. John simply put on a coat over his pyjamas, jumped in his car and drove to the Bromley and Kentish Times car park.

He strode into the editorial office just as the young lady and I were getting rather intimate. When she saw another man arriving in his pyjamas she got the wrong impression. The result was that she quickly adjusted her clothing and fled!

But those were great days. I was editing the sports pages and covering the matches of the local amateur football club Bromley.

They had a very forceful chairman called Charlie King, with whom I had a few run-ins. I remember covering one of their games at Clapton where they started with a depleted side because two of their players arrived at the ground after the kick-off.

I saw it as a very good story and went into the dressing room afterwards to interview the two late arrivals. King followed me in and was so furious, because he felt the story would paint the club in a bad light, that he tore up my notebook!

Those days prepared me well for later dealing with big name chairmen Ron Noades at Crystal Palace and Brentford, Martin Edwards at Manchester United and Ken Bates at Chelsea. None of them made me as apprehensive as the formidable Charlie King.

I have learned not to be intimidated by anyone, no matter how famous or overbearing they might be and how big the occasion. Even being in the Press Box for Millwall's last match at the old Den, and having seats hurled at us by irate fans, didn't phase me!

My first wife Stephanie and I were not party

animals, but we got used to attending all sorts of dinners, dances and functions.

As I got older I mingled more with celebrities, but my second wife Heather was at first very nervous about the prospect of meeting them.

I found this out while I was courting her when I took her to a dinner in honour of George Best at the Savoy Hotel in The Strand.

Heather and I were supposed to meet in the Savoy's reception area, but she was so apprehensive about the possibility of bumping into some of the star-studded guests that she waited for me outside the hotel. Fortunately, when we later talked to Michael Parkinson and his wife Mary, they immediately put her at ease with their friendly manner.

CHAPTER THIRTY-ONE

# EVEN THE CAST CRITICISED DURBRIDGE PLAY

Chatting with celebrities can be fun - the trick is knowing what questions to ask them if you want to find out anything meaningful!

Anyone can mingle with big name actors by going to first nights of London productions – I found myself talking to Roger Lloyd Pack, Arlene Phillips, Kate Thornton and Holly Willoughby in the bar at one production alone – or joining a 'friends group' at your local theatre.

In Eastbourne, the normal custom of The Friends of the Devonshire Park Theatre has been to invite the cast to have drinks with members in the bar after the first night performance.

This has resulted in myself and other members having enjoyable chats with the likes of Susan Penhaligon, Joanne Heywood, Joanna Van Gyseghem, Liza Goddard, former Dr Who Colin Baker, Susie Amy, Denis Lill, Brian Capron and two great blokes with whom I have kept in touch - former pop star-turned-actor Mark Wynter and Neil Roberts.

During these get-togethers you can find out some interesting titbits of information. For example, Mark Wynter, who I had first met, together with fellow singer Helen Shapiro, when they were in the hit parade in the 1960's, shared some amusing backstage stories with me recently, while Neil Roberts told me how his son Thomas had written a cookery book with a difference called 'Meals In The Limelight' containing recipes from celebrities. It tells you about what Arnold Schwarzenegger has for breakfast, Keira Knightley's favourite cake and Judi Dench's ideal dessert.

Of course, when having brief chats with celebrities it is easy to say the wrong thing and perhaps dent their egos. I forgot that Roger Lloyd-Pack, best known for his TV roles in 'Only Fools And Horses' and 'The Vicar of Dibley', had been in the film 'Harry Potter and the Goblet of

Colin Baker meets members of
The Friends of the Devonshire Park Theatre

Fire' and referred to a completely different film. But like, Susie Amy, who I mistakenly called by her surname, he let me off with a smile.

The same applied with Colin Baker, who was playing the role of Inspector Morse in 'House of Ghosts' when I met him. He picked me up on a malapropism, but said he had a forgiving nature, as he seemed to prove previously by touring with his ex-wife Liza Goddard in 'She Stoops To Conquer' in 2008.

Some touring productions include several well known actors, as was the case with 'Fatal Encounter' by Francis Durbridge, which came to Devonshire Park Theatre in September 2009.

All smiles from Anita Harris

It starred Nicholas Ball ('EastEnders' and 'Hazell'), singer-actress Anita Harris and Neil Stacy ('Duty Free'). Unfortunately, it was not one of Durbridge's best thrillers - and even the cast admitted it lacked credibility. My review in the

Brighton Argus was actually kinder than the opinions the actors expressed!

Friends chairman Harry Lederman introduced me to celebrities at other Friends functions, including a very pleasant Kevin Pallister, the star of West End musical 'Blood Brothers'.

It was Harry who arranged for the film premiere of my comedy 'Hacking It' to be shown at the Winter Garden Theatre, Eastbourne, after he and fellow movie maker Alan Tutt had filmed it. Executive director Alan G. Baker has since sent it to television companies as a suggested pilot for a sitcom so some day you may even get the chance to view it.

If you want to see the DVD, starring Dean Matthews, Mandy Lloyd and other actors from Seaford Little Theatre, get in touch with me at tflood04@yahoo.co.uk It is a real hoot!

Hopefully 'Hacking It' will enjoy more screen time than my wife Heather was given as an extra in the film Brighton Rock - blink and you miss her!

Since Heather and I became authors, we have made ourselves available to give talks and do book readings and signings.

My biggest piece of advice to would-be authors is: be ruthless in rewriting your work and be persistent with approaches to publishers. Remember that J.K. Rowling was rejected many times by publishers before getting her first Harry

Potter book accepted - so don't give up.
You can help yourself greatly by getting others to read your manuscript and offer advice. Then be prepared to amend it, and, when you are finally satisfied, send it off to more than one publisher (after finding out first that they accept unsolicited manuscripts).
And landing a publishing deal is only the beginning for an author! These days authors are expected to carry out a lot of their own marketing, including arranging book signings, readings and talks and requesting support from their friends on Facebook etc!
It is also important for authors to seek out celebrities or 'experts' in the subject they have written about, and ask them to endorse their books, as Heather and I have done.
As I mentioned previously, my fantasy adventure book 'The Secret Potion' has been recommended by actress June Whitfield as an ideal follow up to Harry Potter, while Heather's books for younger children, 'Mousey Mousey and the Witches' Spells' and 'Giant Sticker Monster and Other Children's Stories', have been compared favourably by reviewers to Beatrix Potter and Enid Blyton.
Authors can also approach their local Member of Parliament or Mayor to launch or endorse their books - Eastbourne MP Stephen Lloyd and Mayor Carolyn Heaps have both made glowing

tributes to our books.

Always be on the lookout for marketing opportunities. This includes putting yourself on youtube. You can see Heather and I giving everyone a laugh on our youtube videos - and me getting blown up in the process. Do search for TonyxFlood - otherwise you will get my alter ego, a wrestler named Tony Flood who lacks my speed and agility!

CHAPTER THIRTY-TWO

# HOW £50 TROPHIES GAINED US A PRICELESS TV PLUG

Being editor of Football Monthly, Britain's oldest soccer magazine, was a great honour, even though I took over in its declining years.

At one time Charles Buchan's Football Monthly, which was first brought out in September, 1951, was a best seller. But, following its relaunch as 'Football' in July 1974, circulation fell, despite changing the name back to 'Football Monthly' in November 1980.

This was no fault of the then editor Tony Pullein. The plain fact was that the magazine no longer had the market to itself and was up against the power of IPC - by 1971 both Shoot and Goal magazines were the market leaders with 220,000 weekly sales each.

After taking over as editor, I tried to revive Football Monthly's fortunes on a limited budget by making it harder-hitting and brighter, while still retaining it's credibility as a reliable source of information and quality features.

The problem was that we had no money to spend on big promotions or advertising campaigns as our rivals did.

So I came up with the idea of getting free exposure

on at least one major television network. I launched the Football Monthly TV awards for soccer presenters and commentators.

The first awards went to well respected commentator Brian Moore and presenter Matt Lorenzo, both of whom were on ITV. I approached their ITV bosses and arranged for the channel to let me present the awards as part of one of their programmes.

As a result Football Monthly obtained TV exposure worth thousands of pounds for the cost of the two trophies I purchased at a local shop – a total outlay of about £50.

I showed my commitment to the magazine by becoming joint owner of it with Brenda and Peter Rea, who had previously ran it with Peter's partner Graham Buttenshaw. We came up with a variety of schemes to try to promote and improve it, but the odds were stacked against us as a small publisher.

For example, several WHSmith stores refused to display our magazine - despite the fact they had regular orders for it from some of our loyal readers.

In their wisdom, the managers of these branches kept copies of Football Monthly in their cabinets until they were collected by those who had ordered them – but did not think that other sales might be achieved if they put some additional copies on their shelves!

Trying to overcome these sort of problems and do the whole editorial operation on my own, with just a small, faithful group of underpaid freelance writers to call upon, wasn't easy. There was not enough money coming in to pay me a full-time salary so I worked for Football Monthly part-time while holding down another job elsewhere.

I say 'part-time', but as Press day neared each month I would find myself working until up to three o'clock in the morning to get everything done on time.

We eventually ran into financial difficulties and sold the magazine. Unfortunately, the new owners, and those who succeeded them, could not break the stranglehold of the IPC giants, either.

Peter Rea and I tried to keep Football Monthly alive by reacquiring it and then selling it to Ken Bates at Chelsea Football Club in 1995. Ken devoted time and money in an attempt to breathe new life into the magazine, but it is now a collectors' item.

Those copies printed in the early years under the name of Charles Buchan, the former Arsenal and Sunderland star, who edited Football Monthly until June 1974, are particularly valuable. The first issue has changed hands for £85 – pretty good considering that it originally cost just one shilling and six pence (seven and a half pence)!

CHAPTER THIRTY-THREE

# CHARLTON'S 'DI STEFANO'

So who was my all time favourite sports heroes? Ali and Best are joint second but my absolute favourite was someone many people will not even have heard of.

He was Stuart Leary, a footballer with Charlton Athletic, the team I followed as a boy, and a cricketer with Kent.

Leary was a deep lying centre-forward in the mould of Real Madrid legend Alfredo Di Stefano. He was a prolific marksman and was Charlton's all-time record scorer with 153 goals from 1953 to 1962, but it was his great vision and inch-perfect passing that made him so outstanding.

For many years Stuart, a South African, managed to fit in his summer job of playing cricket for Kent with his football career. But when Frank Hill became Charlton manager he didn't like the fact that Leary would start pre-season football training late while completing the cricket season.

A battle of wills resulted. It seemed Charlton would do the unthinkable and part with their star player due mainly to what many fans perceived as their manager's stubbornness.

Stuart went home to South Africa and the English Press could not contact him. So I posted off a letter to him, containing a list of questions about the situation, and he sent me back a full and frank reply.

I sold the story to the national Press and, for good measure, added that the words 'Hill must go' were daubed on the wall outside the Charlton ground.

I had let my feelings as a devoted supporter conflict with my journalist judgement. But to ensure my story was true, I then went down to The Valley at the dead of night, found a suitable wall and wrote the offending words on it.

It almost broke my heart and Leary's when in 1962 Stuart eventually moved to QPR where he never quite showed the same level of brilliance he had consistently displayed at Charlton.

Despite being South African born, Leary had appeared for the England Under 23 team, but was prevented from representing the senior side by the Football Association, who banned non-English-born players from representing the national team

Stuart was not just a great player - he was also a wonderful bloke. So it was a tragedy when he died in controversial circumstances at the age of 55.

His body was discovered dead on Table Mountain in South Africa on August 23, 1988 - four days after his car had been found abandoned.

Charlton have one claim to fame that even the

likes of Manchester United and Chelsea cannot match - they produced the greatest comeback in football history by amazingly rallying from 5-1 down to beat Huddersfield 7-6 with 10 men in the old Division Two at The Valley in 1957.

Only 12,535 people saw this incredible match and I was not among them as it was one of the few home matches I missed that season as a devoted 14-year-old fan.

Charlton had lost centre-half and skipper Derek Ufton, who was carried off with a dislocated shoulder in the 17th minute, and nobody gave them a chance when they trailed 5-1 to Bill Shankly's Huddersfield with 28 minutes remaining.

But, with the immaculate Leary pulling the strings, and Johnny Summers, a journeyman left-winger, playing the game of his life to score five goals after changing his disintegrating boots, Charlton went 6-5 ahead.

Four minutes from the end Huddersfield drew level at 6-6 when a shot from Stan Howard was deflected into his own net by John Hewie, and it seemed the Robins would be denied a sensational win.

But in the dying seconds Summers crossed for John 'Buck' Ryan to score his second goal of the game and give Charlton an unbelievable victory.

Tragically, the Robins' hero Summers died of cancer within five years of his epic performance.

During my time as a sports writer I had a couple of run-ins with former Charlton manager Alan Curbishley because of my criticisms of his striker Carl Leaburn's lack of goals.

Leaburn became a cult figure as a striker who rarely scored - his record was a meagre 57 goals in 388 league appearances with Charlton, Northampton and MK Dons!

A hard-hitting match report I wrote for Sunday paper The People particularly upset Curbishley. He took the opportunity to criticise what I had said, while defending Leaburn and his own team selection, in an article in the local Charlton newspaper the South East London Mercury.

What Curbishley did not seem to consider was that the Mercury might offer me the right of reply. They actually invited me to give my views and used them as the back page lead story the following week.

The main point I made was that Leaburn might be a good target man, but his goals record was so poor he failed to reach double figures most seasons, which meant his strike partner would probably need to score at least 30 a season to make Charlton a successful side and this was simply not practical. I don't think Curbishley was best pleased, but hopefully he accepted that I felt as strongly about the matter as he did!

CHAPTER THIRTY-FOUR

# JAMES CRACKNELL RISKED HIS LIFE

THE first story I ever had published turned out to be a lie!

It was back in the early 1960's and I had just landed my first job as a junior reporter on the Lewisham Borough News, but still had a few weeks to go before completing my education at the South East London Day College, which was also in Lewisham.

A party of students from the college went on a day trip (to Oxford, if I remember correctly). Two of the boys in our group took a punt out on the river and came back soaking wet from head to foot.

They told us how a small girl had fallen into the river and they had dived in to save her. So I wrote a story for the Borough News about local boys rescuing drowning girl and they printed it on their front page.

Only then did the two boys reveal that they had made up the tale about the girl in the river. They confessed to me that they were fooling around on a punt and fell in, but were so scared of the master in charge that they invented a story about them being heroes!

My early days as a journalist were spent covering

Greenwich court, flower shows, community meetings and the like. My most 'exciting' story at that time was the revelation at a rather boring meeting that coal merchants doused their sacks in water to make them heavier!

When the official sitting next to me saw me writing franticly, he hissed: "You can't print that - it's dynamite!"

Fortunately the Sports Editor John Richards took me under his wing and soon I was reporting on Charlton, Crystal Palace and Millwall. When he left I took over his job and, at 19, was probably the youngest sports editor in the country.

My career path took me to the Kentish Times Series, the Slough Observer Series, the Sunday

Tony dishes out awards once again with help from Trevor Brooking (L) and David Lloyd (R)

Express as a part-timer, the Lancashire Evening Telegraph and Star, Football Monthly, Sunday Sport, Fleet Street News Agency, Sky Television, the Richmond and Twickenham Times Series, the News of the World and The People.

I still keep my hand in as Managing Director of Sportsworld Communications, but I have retired from full time journalism and now spend most of my time as an author and theatre critic.

As I said earlier, the most emotive story I have ever written was my exclusive interview with Liverpool goalkeeper Bruce Grobbelaar the day after he played for Liverpool against Nottingham Forest in the Hillsborough Disaster which killed 96 people at Sheffield Wednesday's football ground on April 15, 1989.

I did not report on Liverpool matches, but obtained other exclusive interviews with some of their players and former manager Bob Paisley.

My interview with Paisley came in 1988 after I left Sunday Sport, together with the two full-time members of my staff, in protest at the paper's weird news stories having an adverse effect on our sports coverage.

The three of us had been phoning around Fleet Street asking if there were any suitable jobs, and this included a conversation with the Sports Editor of The Sun, who had no vacancies.

Immediately afterwards I landed the job as Sports Editor of Fleet Street News Agency where my main task was to set up a new sports section, producing and marketing stories to national papers in competition with vastly larger agencies such as the Press Association and Exchange Telegraph.

What I needed was a big exclusive story to get us off to a good start. So I contacted Paisley, who in 1983 had completed nine glorious years as Liverpool manager during which he led them to six League titles, three European Cups, one UEFA Cup, three League Cups, five Community Shields and a UEFA Super Club.

The man regarded by many as the greatest Liverpool manager of all time did not usually give in depth interviews, but he made an exception with me. I suggested that he hit back at criticisms of the club and himself, and I gleefully contacted every Fleet Street sports editor to offer them the story.

They all took my calls with the exception of the Sun's Sports Editor. Perhaps he thought I was still trying to persuade him to give me a job, but the upshot was that I gave the story to everyone apart from him. The next morning it made headlines almost everywhere, and The Sun felt obliged to run a follow-up story a day later.

Interviews with England bosses Bobby Robson, Howard Wilkinson and Terry Venables, and Brian Barwick when he first took over as the FA Chief Executive in 2005, brought me further big

Terry Butcher was gentle with Tony...

Martin Allen less so.

exclusives.

Competing against the whole of Fleet Street wasn't easy because national newspapers, television and other agencies had far more staff, better resources and, in many cases, more contacts. But I obtained a fair share of column inches.

I made endless telephone calls to achieve other headline-making interviews with managers such as Arsenal's George Graham, Manchester United's Alex Ferguson, Charlton's Lennie Lawrence, Steve Gritt and Alan Curbishley and Spurs' Terry Venables and Peter Shreeve. Others who have given me their time and assistance with stories include Don Howe, David Pleat, Steve Coppell, Brentford's opinionated managers Martin Allen and Terry Butcher, former Liverpool star Tommy Smith, and, of course, Tommy Docherty.

Questioning football club chairmen also brought me some great stories, especially Ron Noades during the time he was being hounded by fans at Brentford over spending costs and the threat of losing their beloved Griffin Park ground.

My relationship with Ken Bates while he was at Chelsea was rather different. He gave me more cash than quotes!

Ken was very interested in the fact that I was editor and co-owner of Football Monthly, Britain's oldest soccer magazine.

We got talking about the fact that the magazine was having financial difficulties, and the result was that Bates actually bought Football Monthly from me and my partner Peter Rea. He kept us on as consultants and treated us very fairly, even extending my contract. So presumably he thought our ideas had some merit because Ken doesn't suffer fools lightly!

I won't bore you by listing the countless personalties from other sports I have interviewed, but let me share with you my surprise at hearing how rowing star James Cracknell risked his life in the pursuit of glory.

He told me that winning gold medals at the Sydney 2000 and Athens 2004 Olympics were a walk in the park compared with conquering the Atlantic in the world's toughest rowing race.

Cracknell revealed: "Driving myself to near exhaustion in the Atlantic Rowing Race with Ben Fogle in 2005 after 2,930 miles and 49 days, in which we encountered the worst weather in the history of the event, was a living hell at times.

"We could have lost our lives when the boat was capsized by a giant wave. We wept, fought, played games, grew beards, nursed blisters and sat on agonisingly sore bottoms, but somehow kept rowing."

He added: "It was harder and in many respects a bigger achievement than my double Olympic gold medals, my three world records or my six world titles."

Although Cracknell and Fogle were the first pair home (overall, they were third to finish behind two men's fours), the use of ballast water during the race resulted in them being moved to second position in the pairs.

# EPILOGUE

Working as a journalist certainly wasn't as gruelling as rowing almost 3,000 miles, but it was, nevertheless, a stressful, demanding, very competitive job, requiring me to put in ridiculously long hours.

I benefited from having a great home life as a young man with my wonderful grandparents, Reg and Winifred Burwash, who brought me up, and my mother Mabel, who was always there for me despite having to cope with poor health and her two divorces.

I also enjoyed the support of my first wife Stephanie until our marriage eventually failed, and the marvellous backing given to me in more recent years by my second wife Heather, a gorgeous lady with a smile as big as her heart. The happiest day of my life was when I married Heather in Richmond in 2002, with her son Lee giving her away, my son James being best man and our daughters Joanne and Emma acting as bridesmaids.

My speech got plenty of chuckles, but I was upstaged by the normally shy James, whose ribbing of me and my faults had his sisters Joanne and Tracey in fits of laughter.

Finally, let me urge you all to look on the bright side by referring you to the words of one of the

The happiest day of my life

biggest (literally) sporting heroes I ever met - rugby super star Jonah Lomu.

The giant Newlander, who towered over me at 6ft 5in tall and 19st 10lb, won 63 caps as an All Black and was the Rugby World Cup all-time top try scorer with 15 tries before being struck down by illness and undergoing a kidney transplant in 2004 so that he could play again.

He said: “I had been running straight over people, scoring tries, winning games and having fun. Then I ended up so sick that I couldn’t even run past a little baby. So I’m just glad to be able to enjoy life again and do what I love most.”

Jonah Lomu’s inspirational message is that, if we are not handicapped by poor health, we should be thankful for what we’ve got!

Heather and I certainly try to do that – and we’ve managed to make each other laugh virtually every day since we’ve been together.

Lomu’s words have also encouraged me to carry on playing football with Sovereign Harbour Veterans despite being an overweight 68-year-old!

NEVER GIVE UP!

Jonah bends down to fit in the photo

# MORE INFORMATION ON TONY AND HEATHER FLOOD'S BOOKS

Tony Flood has taken up writing for children and his first novel, The Secret Potion, is a fantasy adventure story about a young girl called Jody Richards who goes in search of her brother after he is kidnapped by an evil wizard.

Jody finds herself taking on not just the wizard but nasty witches, goblins, pixies and possibly the world's most horrific monster.

Heather also writes for young children, with two collections of short stories published - Mousey Mousey and the Witches' Spells and The Giant Sticker Monster and Other Children's Stories.

You can find them on Amazon or look them up on the website of publisher My Voice Publishing at www.mvpub.co.uk where you can obtain signed copies.

Lightning Source UK Ltd.
Milton Keynes UK
UKOW051714160712

196076UK00001B/141/P